BEFORE THE WHITE MAN CAME

Before the
White Man Came

PACIFIC NORTHWEST
INDIAN CULTURE

By

MILDRED JENKINS

Illustrated by

WILL D. JENKINS

BINFORDS & MORT, *Publishers*
PORTLAND, OREGON

Printed in the United States of America
by
Metropolitan Press, Portland, Oregon

DEDICATED
TO MY HUSBAND
FOR HIS HELP AND COMPANIONSHIP

ACKNOWLEDGMENT

SINCERE GRATITUDE is expressed to the Indian friends who so graciously opened their homes, telling their stories and sharing their rare articles of historical interest; who invited me to their ceremonials and made me feel welcome among them. And to the other friends for their fine assistance and encouragement in this work.

FOREWORD

THE TRIBE OF INDIANS used in this book is a composite one whose life and customs are a general picture of the Indians of the Pacific Northwest.

The reaches of this type of Indian life were from the Cascade mountain range westward to the Pacific Ocean; on the north throughout the islands and mainland of southeastern Alaska down along the coast of British Columbia, Washington, and Oregon, touching upper California. This was the land of giant evergreen trees.

In early times there were many different tribes of Indians along the shores of the salt water bays, lakes and rivers, each having a separate language which was often practically unintelligible to other tribes. In many instances the customs and ways of life varied also. But taken in general, these coastal tribes were so similar by nature of environment as to be accepted as a type .... the canoe Indians.

Trading went on among the tribes up and down the coast. To obtain articles which they did not have, one tribe traded with another, and often times re-trading with still another tribe. The Northerners had huge sea-going canoes, jadeite tools and the precious hyakwa shell money. The middle tribes had dried fish and clams to trade. The Southerners had root foods, arrowheads and implements. The tribes from the mountain areas had hides and skins and wool. All had various other materials and articles to trade with one another. And the tribes living near the borders of this giant tree area traded with the Indians who had still different ways of life and so obtained articles not to be had in their own home place. They in turn traded with their neighbors, thus spreading and intermixing the crafts of the Northwest Indians. The natural routes used in those early times later became modern east-west arteries of travel and trade.

It is an accepted fact that many early customs of the Indians of the Northwestern area are disputed, both among the Indians themselves and among students of ethnology. There are few records, the information at hand having been transmitted from generation to generation in tribal teachings.

In gathering material for this book the author talked with members of various tribes, old people whenever possible, and those younger ones interested in preserving their cultural backgrounds; attended ceremonies which harkened back to the olden days; sat all night long in dark Smokehouses with only the light of flaming wood fires while the dancing and vibrant song of the drums carried performers and spectators alike back into the days when the Indian was alone in this great country . . . before the white man came. For days afterwards the echo of the drums rang in our ears and the sensitive music sang in our hearts.

An attempt has been made to recapture the life of the Indian before the interference of white influence. Some points were intentionally omitted, always keeping in mind that the purpose of this work is to present for the use of children a general picture of original Indian life in the Pacific Northwest.

CONTENTS

INSIDE OF HOUSE

Chapter I

TIDEWATER FAMILY

SWALOOS AND MALITSA were Indian children who lived in a small village on the shore of a winding salty inland sea. The Indians called this great inlet *whulge*. That was before the white men came.

Many different tribes of Indians lived in villages along the shores, from the lower end of what is now Alaska, down through British Columbia, Washington and Oregon, on to touch upper California. This area reached eastward to the first mountain range, now called the Cascades. These people lived in very much the same manner. They were canoe Indians, and their main food was fish.

(1)

Not all the villages were on the salt water beaches. Some were inland, on fresh water lakes, along the river valleys, and back near the mountains. The villages were often far apart but the people visited each other now and then, to trade or to attend special potlatch parties. Sometimes they made war on one another. The languages of the many tribes were usually different, so much of their trading was by sign language.

Silvery rain fell from the sky many days of the year and watered this land. Evergreen trees grew to great size, cedars with gracefully sweeping limbs, pitchy fir, hemlock, yew, and spruce trees. There were also maples, alders, cottonwoods, birches, and cherry trees. But to the Indians the cedars were most important. From the cedars they got bark for their clothing, boards for their houses, wood for their dugout canoes, and many other useful articles.

Swaloos, the grandson of a chief, counted his age by the fingers on both his hands but his sister Malitsa was younger. She had two fingers over on the second hand after she counted her age. When time passed so they counted their ages by all their fingers and then another hand, these childhood names would be changed. They would then be given their grownup names.

It was the custom for an old relative to choose the final name. This name was often that of an ancestor who had been greatly admired, and would be an ideal for the young person to grow toward. The father would give a party and invite many people. There would be feasting and dancing and games. From that time on, the young man or woman would be known by the new name and would try to be worthy of the honor.

But Swaloos and Malitsa must wait a few years before the time would come for their grownup names.

These children lived in a long cedar house with their parents and grandparents. The house belonged to their grandfather, Chief Carver-of-Wood, who was the leader of his tribe. The house was divided into sections by walls of cedar boards and large hanging cat-tail mats. Uncles and aunts and their families lived in the various sections, for only relatives of the Chief lived in that house. Other people of the village lived in smaller houses. Sometimes there might be more than one large house to a village.

The man who owned a large house was considered wealthy. The tools of the Indians were crude and it took a long time to cut all the cedar trees for posts and poles, and to split the boards to build such a big house.

The tools used by the Indians before the coming of the white men had to be made from what nature offered them. They made crude stone implements by grinding or pecking one kind of stone against another until a tool took shape. They saved certain bones and the antlers from the animals they killed for food. They made chisels and wedges from elk horn; also wedges from stone and hard wood knots, mauls from stone and hard wood, knives from bone and shell.

With these crude tools the Indians cut down cedar trees and prepared poles and posts to build their houses. Large log posts were set in the ground. Then the great beams and poles to form the building were chiseled and fit together for strength. Long, wide boards were split from cedar trees by using the elkhorn chisels, wedges and mauls. The boards were placed on end to form the side walls and were held in place with wooden pegs and cedar root thongs. Long boards were used for the roof, too. These were placed with overlapping edges to shed water. Rocks were put on for weights in times of wind. There was a space left in the roof for the smoke from their fires to escape.

Most of the inside posts of the house had carvings of family stories and legends. The children were told these

(3)

stories over and over to remind them to grow up to be fine people so the family would be proud of them too. Family honor was important to these Indians.

Some day Swaloos hoped to become chief of his tribe, but he must deserve the honor. If the people of the village decided that the man who was in line to be the next chief was not worthy, they would choose another man of the family instead. The boy knew this well. He tried to remember it always in his work or play. He wanted very much to follow in the footsteps of his grandfather.

Malitsa was being taught woman's work, and to be kind, to walk proudly, to speak gently. Some day she might become the wife of a chief and she must be able to fit into such an honored place.

The Indians in the region of great cedars wore clothing which the women made from cedar bark. They also had some clothes from skins but usually those were saved for special wear.

Spring and summer were the seasons for gathering in supplies. Fish were caught from the sea and dried over smoky fires. Clams were dug from the tide flats, dried, and stored. Berries were gathered and dried for winter use. Meat was cured over the fires. Much of the foods the Indians would need during the winter was gathered, dried, and stored in baskets on high shelves inside their houses. Rushes and barks, strong roots and slender limbs were gathered for winter weaving.

When summer was gone and the fall rains came to feed the mighty evergreens, the Indians worked under shelter. Sometimes the icy north wind froze the rain and snow fell and winter's cold nipped at the brown bodies.

The Indians were busy during the winter season. The mothers and grandmothers wove baskets and mats. They pounded and shredded cedar bark, and made new clothing for the family. They twisted cord and made fish nets. The girls watched, helped and learned.

The men carved. They made bows and arrows. They carved bowls and spoons and other articles from maple wood, and hewed canoes from cedar trees they had felled. They made bone spears and hooks for fishing. The boys stayed with them, helped, and learned manly tasks.

The materials had all been gathered from the woods or the water or the earth, and the Indians must shape them to meet their needs.

Swaloos and Malitsa had reached the age of learning. Swaloos liked learning to make arrowheads and knives, bows and arrows, and even hewing out a great cedar log to make a canoe. Malitsa was happy now that Grandmother really showed her how to make baskets and headbands and mats. And Mother let her help prepare the food for their meals. The children were now old enough to go across the bay to dig clams and upriver to hunt, and to gather berries and basket grasses. They found each day new and interesting.

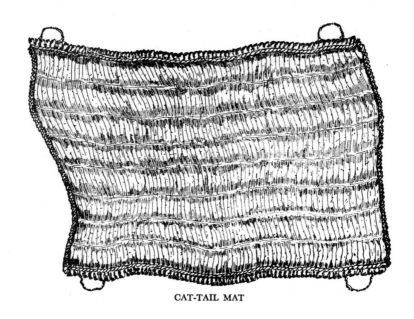

CAT-TAIL MAT

Chapter II

THE DAY BEGINS

VERY EARLY one morning a loud noise waked Swaloos. He opened his eyes quickly. He knew that his grandfather was calling the family to get up.

Every morning Grandfather was up first. He took his stick and rapped on the cedar boards of the wall. The blows made enough noise to rouse all the household. They must get up immediately. The sound of the stick said to Swaloos, "Get up! Get up!" But the sound of the stick soon died away.

A soft voice inside the boy's ear said, "Snuggle down in bed. Feel how warm it is. I am your friend, the bed. I will keep you warm."

Swaloos snuggled down under the warm cover. He did

(6)

not want to get up now. He closed his eyes to sleep a little longer.

The bed was a low shelf along the wall of the house. It was wide and made of cedar boards, with a padding of cattail mats so the boards would not feel so hard. The covers were skins and blankets of goat wool and cedar bark woven together. Mother had woven them with Grandmother's help.

Malitsa hurried to join her mother, Woman-With-Busy-Hands. Together they went along the path toward the creek which emptied into the salt water close by the village. It was the custom for the women and girls to bathe in the fresh water of the stream. Then men and boys bathed in the salt water.

As they came to the creek a bird flew up and away, scolding loudly. "The bluejay is a noisy fellow," Mother said, "but his feathers make beautiful decorations." They heard many other bird calls after the bluejay's scolding had died away. Small birds twittered in the woods. The harsh cawing of black crows was heard from the beach. The shrill cry of the silvery seagull came to them as he flew above the salt water hunting for fish. They saw a kingfisher in his blue-gray coat and white collar sitting on a limb above the stream. The dark feathers of his hood stood on end and then like a flash he was off upstream. Malitsa and her mother bathed, and dried themselves with moss they found close by.

On the way back toward their house Malitsa saw the shining white petal face of a trillium beside the path and ran to pick it.

"Oh, do not pick the little white blossom," said Mother. "It would be sad. A tear would come on the broken stem and its brown bulb-root would die for it could not make its seeds. It grows to make seeds. Let the trillium live to tell of spring."

The child felt ashamed and knew she would never again

want to pick the flower with three white petals and three green leaves.

When they returned to their house Mother stirred among the ashes where their fires were always made and found some live coals. She put some shredded cedar bark on the coals to feed them and soon a tiny blaze sprang up.

Inside the house the sleeping Swaloos stirred, then his eyes popped open. Suddenly he remembered what Grandfather had told him. It was not manly to lie in bed in the morning. One should hop out of bed and be wide awake. Grandfather had told him that the bed says, "I am your friend. Do not leave me. I will keep you warm."

Swaloos knew his bed had said just that to him and he had heeded it. He knew it was saying that to him now. The bed felt so good, he wanted to stay there.

"A boy must be stronger than his bed," Grandfather had said. "He must get right up and leave it. He must show the bed it cannot hold him back."

Swaloos was ashamed. He had listened to the bed. He had let it be the stronger.

"I will show it," cried Swaloos, hopping out. "I will show that bed it cannot hold me. I will never let it hold me back again. I am going to be strong and manly like my father and my grandfather."

Swaloos came out of the house into the sunshine. The bright light made him blink his eyes. Usually he was up before the sun came over the big tree tops. This morning he was late because of his weakness.

Woman - With - Busy - Hands was kneeling beside the morning fire and Malitsa stood nearby. Her face was clean and shining and her hair was neatly combed.

The boy knew now that he was very late. His mother and sister had already been to the creek to bathe. Man-With-Piercing-Eyes, his father, must also have finished bathing. Swaloos would have to go alone. He had been so

(8)

proud when he had become old enough to bathe with his father.

Mother did not scold Swaloos. She just looked at him. The boy knew she was not pleased and he knew it made her sad when he did not act as the grandson of a chief should. His father would not be pleased to hear of this.

The boy said to his mother, "I am very sorry. Never again will I allow the bed to be stronger than I am."

Mother nodded and smiled a little. She felt sure that her son had learned a lesson. His shame showed on his face.

Swaloos hurried down to the salt water to bathe. He would bathe long and well, and wash away his weakness. He would rub his brown body hard with shredded cedar bark, hard enough to make it sting. He would be stronger when he had finished.

Chapter III

THE CHILDREN LEARN TO HELP

MALITSA GATHERED some dry twigs. She was careful how she placed them on the small flames, for she was learning to feed a fire. Many times she had watched Mother and now she was old enough to help.

The twigs must be placed just right to make the fire burn quickly. It was the work of the women to tend the fires. They must learn to coax quick heat from the flames. If a fire burned slowly with little heat, the other women thought her slow and lazy.

Malitsa wanted to learn the secret of a quick fire and she was doing very well. Her fire was crackling and blazing merrily.

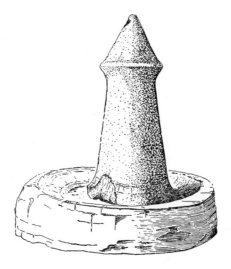

STONE PESTLE AND BOWL

Woman-With-Busy-Hands was preparing the food for breakfast. Malitsa watched while her mother ground some dried venison. Venison is meat from deer. Mother held a shaped grinding stone called a pestle in one hand and with the other hand she steadied a stone bowl, crushing the dried venison between the pestle and bowl. When Mother had crushed enough meat, Malitsa brought her the fat. The meat and fat were then mixed together and heated over the fire.

The girl spread the eating mat on the ground and set the shell dishes for the family. She called them to eat, for the great maple bowl of the good breakfast was now ready. First Grandfather and Father dipped with their large clam shells. It was the custom for the men of the family to begin to eat before all others. Then the women and children could eat.

When the meal was over, Malitsa gathered the bowls. She cleaned them with moss and shredded cedar bark to be ready for the next meal, and set them away. They would not have another meal until evening. At noontime they only nibbled some dried food.

After the men had left the house to go to their work, Malitsa helped her mother. She straightened the mats on the beds and then brushed the hard-padded dirt floor with a cedar limb. Mother climbed up to the storage shelf to examine the food which was stored in baskets. She must examine it every few days to be sure it was not spoiling.

"You may play now," Mother told the girl after the morning work was done.

Malitsa quickly ran outside and called to her friend, Smiling-Girl, who lived nearby. They took their cedar bark dolls and went to the home of Swinging-Fringes who had a small baby.

"May we come in?" the girls asked softly at the door. They spoke quietly for the baby might be asleep.

"Come in," called Swinging-Fringes. "Baby is awake."

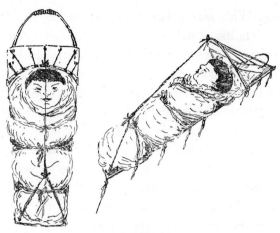

BABY BOARDS

The baby was on his baby board and he smiled at the two
girls. His smile was funny for he had no teeth. Swinging-
Fringes moved the baby board to a mat and then untied the
baby to let him kick and rest. She rubbed his legs and arms
and back. The girls played with him. Then they watched
while Swinging-Fringes fixed shredded cedar bark to make
the board comfortable for the baby. She put him on it again
and laced the deer skin covering firmly so he could not fall
out. Soon he was fast asleep and the girls tiptoed away.

Swaloos had gone out with his father that morning. It
was spring and Father was finishing a beautiful dugout
canoe. It seemed to Swaloos that his father had worked on
this canoe for such a long time.

The work had begun back in the woods where the cedar
tree had grown for so many years. Father had chosen a
perfect tree for his canoe and before felling it he had said a
prayer. He promised the tree. "I will make you live again."

Then had begun the long and tedious work of felling
the big tree. Father had used his chisels and wedges and
mauls. The wedges had been driven into the tree at the
place where Father wanted to cut it off. He had pounded the

wedges in with a maul, a wedge above and a wedge below. Then the piece between the wedges was split out by hammering on the chisel with a maul until the wood turned loose. Over and over and over this was done until the groove was broad and deep. After many days of labor the tree was ready to fall. Father knew which way he wanted the tree to fall and he had shaped the great notch to make the tree fall in that direction.

Sometimes a canoe tree was felled by using fire. To protect the huge trunk from burning too much, a thick ring of wet sticky mud was plastered on the tree. Below the ring of mud the tree trunk was set on fire. The fire must be guarded and tended with a watchful eye because of the danger of spreading to other trees. And because cedar burns so readily. Now and again the fire would be allowed to smoulder while the deeply charred wood was chopped and scraped away.

CROSS SECTION OF ROUGHED OUT CANOE DEVELOPMENT

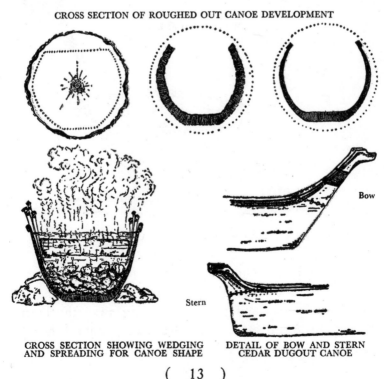

CROSS SECTION SHOWING WEDGING
AND SPREADING FOR CANOE SHAPE

Bow

Stern

DETAIL OF BOW AND STERN
CEDAR DUGOUT CANOE

(13)

Then the fire was kindled and again set to work for the Indian. This went on until the flames had finally eaten so deep into the base of the giant tree that it went crashing to the ground.

But Father had not used the fire method this time.

After the great tree was down, Father made sure it had not been damaged in the fall. Then he measured off the length he wanted for his canoe. Allowing extra length for working, he again cut through the tree to remove the unwanted section. Then Father began to hew the tree into shape.

Swaloos had watched day after day while his father chipped away the wood with a stone adz. Slowly, so very

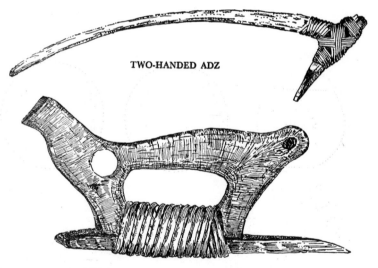

TWO-HANDED ADZ

AN ADZ WITH WOODEN HANDLE AND STONE BIT

slowly, the tree lost its shape and the form of a canoe came into being. The inside was hollowed out by wedging and splitting; by fire and then by scraping away the burned wood. This was done over and over and over until the shell of the canoe was nearly thin enough.

When Father was ready other men of the village helped him. They brought the rough canoe from the woods to a place near their home. There it was to be finished. It was braced to sit even.

Father had filled it with water, and left it until the water had soaked into the wood. Then the water must be heated to steam and shape the canoe.

The children carried wood for fires. Mother tended the fires and heated stones. Uncles helped Father put the red hot stones into the water to make it boil. The boiling water steamed the wood and it began to soften. Carefully they wedged strong sticks across and inside the dugout, which forced the sides to bulge outward. As the canoe widened, new sets of sticks were added, each set a little longer than those already used. When the canoe was stretched as wide as they wanted it to be, the water was allowed to cool and then emptied. The sticks held the canoe in its curved shape until the sides dried, and after that it never changed.

Father was now doing the finishing alone. He chipped and smoothed the sides. Swaloos wanted to help but his strokes were not like those of his father. Sometimes he dug too deep with the tool and at other times the tool slipped off without cutting the wood. It took years of practice to make every stroke count. After the chipping was done, Father used polishing stones to smooth the wood.

Finally the canoe was ready for the ends. The front end, or bow, was shaped like an animal head. Father said to his son, "This is the new life for the tree. Now I give it life again."

The back end, or stern, had a plainer piece added. Swaloos watched his father use hot pitch and wooden pegs to make the ends fast to the canoe. Father was pleased with the beautiful lines of his dugout.

Each day Swaloos went to work with his father. He watched and helped whenever he could. After the canoe

SWALOOS HELPING FATHER WORK ON CEDAR DUGOUT CANOES

was shaped it must be painted. Father built a fire near it and burned pitch wood. The black smoke from the burning pitch blackened the outside of the dugout. Father took handfuls of shredded cedar bark and rubbed the black into the new wood. He rubbed and rubbed until the canoe was colored black.

Mother made some paint by mashing dried salmon eggs and adding enough water to make a soft glue. She mixed crushed charcoal in it to make a black paint. Now Father covered the canoe with this paint, and used cedar bark to rub it into the wood. When the paint dried it became very hard, and so protected the canoe from wind and water.

"I have finished on time," Father said. "Very soon the spring fishing season will be here."

Swaloos was proud of the canoe for it was the first time he had ever helped with the building of one.

One day soon they would hold a ceremony and with the help of his relatives, Father would slide the long cedar dugout out into the green seawater to be ready for fishing. The head on the bow would rise on the waves and become as a thing alive.

DIGGING STICK

BUNDLE OF DRYING STICKS

DIGGING STICK

Chapter IV

A JOURNEY

EVERYONE WAS BUSY. Many families were preparing to move to the clam beds where they would stay while they dried a supply of clams.

Mother was packing the things they would need. She took the ironwood digging sticks, and the small bundle of drying sticks, which were also of ironwood. She brought out the clam baskets. She rolled up the cat-tail sleeping mats, and the larger cat-tail mats for their shelter. Malitsa and Swaloos helped their mother.

Father had the large traveling canoe ready. He loaded the poles for their shelter. Malitsa and her brother carried things down to the shore, and Father packed the dugout canoe.

At last they were ready to go.

Mother called the children to paint their faces. The boy and girl laughed happily for they liked to be painted. They stood still while Mother rubbed the red grease paint all over their faces. Father rubbed paint on his face, too.

"The paint is to keep the wind and sun from burning your faces," Mother said. "The wind blows across the salt water. It is not good for the skin. It dries and burns. The grease keeps the skin soft."

The children thought the color the most important part of painting.

"We are ready," Father said, and gave the signal to the other families waiting beside their canoes. The Indians took their places quietly. The old people stayed at home but they came down to the water's edge to say good-bye to their relatives. They sang their good luck song. Malitsa and Swaloos waved to their grandmother and grandfather.

FAMILY IN CANOE READY TO TRAVEL
AND MAN'S TRAVELING PADDLE

Dip. Drip. Dip. Drip. The paddles were lifted and lowered into the salt water. Each time the paddle went into the water, the canoe was pushed forward, moving steadily toward the distant island.

The children liked the lifting and lowering motion of the canoe as it rode the swells. They smiled happily, but they did not laugh aloud. Nor did they talk loudly. Indian children were taught to be very quiet, especially when on a journey.

The men kept their canoes close together and watched as

they crossed the water. Sometimes enemies came paddling down from the North in great war canoes. The men must guard against a surprise.

When the great sun hung high overhead, Mother gave the children some dried berries to eat.

Swaloos said, "Thank you, Mother. I am very hungry."

"It is the smell of the salt wind," Mother told him. "The wind scuttles over the salt water gathering healthy ocean smells which make one very hungry. When the sun swings low we will have a good supper."

The journey seemed very long and the children became tired. They had sat still many hours. How they wished they might stretch their legs. But the canoe was piled with mats, baskets, and other necessary things leaving no room to stretch.

Now and then a big fish came close to the dugout. They saw great numbers of tiny fish swimming together. They passed over beds of seaweed. Long snake-like kelp floated here and there. The children remembered how they had found kelp and green seaweed washed up on the beach at home. The waves had carried these deep-sea plants in to the shore. Now the children saw them floating far out on the green water.

They looked ahead and the blue island finally seemed much closer.

Soon they could see the trees on the island. The Indians in their canoes had almost reached the clam beds and the children were glad. They wanted to run and run. But they remembered they must not make one sound until Father gave the signal. The canoes floated quietly on the water.

Father shaded his eyes and looked hard at the beach. His eyes moved all along the shore searching for some sign that might mean enemies. He saw no one, nor any canoes pulled up on the beach.

He held up his arm in a signal and one canoe shot ahead

of the others. Two men climbed out on the beach. They went far along the shore in opposite directions looking for foot prints on the sand. All the other Indians waited silently. The men came back to their canoes, then gave a signal that it was safe to land. All the canoes moved in to the beach.

As soon as the bottom of the canoe grated on the sand the children sprang out. They ran and jumped in glee, but they did not shout. It was so good to run again.

The parents began unloading the canoes. They carried the poles and mats up on the beach to a spot which had been chosen to set up the mat houses. Poles were placed, the cat-tail mats spread over them, and fastened on with wooden pins.

The children helped, carrying things from the canoe to the shelters. All the baskets and digging sticks were brought up, and also the dishes and the cooking baskets. The new camp was ready to be their home during the clam digging.

"Where will we dig the clams?" Swaloos asked, looking at the water. "The beach is very narrow."

Mother smiled, "Yes, it looks narrow now but when the tide goes out the beach will be very, very wide. It will be much wider than our beach at home. That is why we came here to dig our winter clams. There are so many more clams to be found."

"I wish we could dig them now," said Swaloos.

"We will dig after the sun sleeps and comes again," Mother told him.

PREPARING CLAM DIGGING PIT

Chapter V

DIGGING AND DRYING CLAMS

WHEN THE GREAT SUN CAME UP over the distant hills beyond the water it surprised the Indians. At home the sun must climb above the tops of the tall trees just behind their houses and the Indians were usually up before the sun. Far back across the water the hills and trees seemed small.

But soon the Indians were up, eager to be at their work. Swaloos looked toward the water and found it had backed away from the beach, leaving a very wide and flat muddy-looking beach. The tide was out.

As soon as breakfast was over, Mother scooped out a pit on the dry sandy beach. "Come children, gather stones," she called.

They gathered stones and put them in the bottom of the pit. Then Mother put some fire into the pit on top of the stones and the children brought wood to make a very hot fire. The stones must be heated.

"Now we will dig the clams," Mother said. "The stones will be hot when we come back."

Mother and Father carried digging sticks of ironwood and took open-weave clam baskets. Swaloos and Malitsa also each carried a basket. They turned their baskets upside-down over their heads and their lively brown eyes peeked through the holes of the open work.

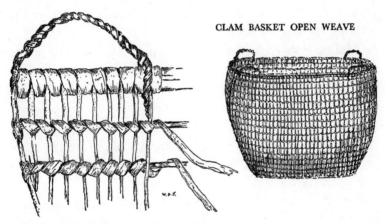

CLAM BASKET OPEN WEAVE

DETAIL OF OPEN WEAVE CLAM BASKET

The sandy mud was warm to their feet and oozed up between their toes as they walked. Little squirts of water popped up at them. The children saw tiny mounds of mud pushed up with a round hole in the center. This meant that sand worms had been at work. Here and there the backing tide had left little pools and the children stopped at some of these to look for the very tiny fish that were sometimes left behind. But the little fish moved quick as a flash and darted away too fast for the brown fingers to catch them.

Father and Mother were far ahead. The children splashed mud as they ran to catch up with them.

Now there were many spurts of water coming up out of the mud. That meant many clams. Mother and Father began to dig. The children gathered the sand-covered clams into the baskets. Digging with a stick was slow and the baskets did not fill very fast. The children tried to dig, too, but they did not do very well.

Finally the baskets were full. The tide was coming in and the Indians waded out into the water with their filled baskets. They swished the baskets back and forth and dipped water over the clams. The water washed the sand off the tightly closed shells and out through the open work of the baskets, leaving the shells clean.

Malitsa looked far along the mud flat. She saw many other children helping their parents. All carried baskets of clams.

They went back to their temporary camp on the beach to empty their baskets.

"Children," said Mother, "we need a lot of seaweed. See it along the beach? The waves brought it in for us. Please bring plenty for me."

The children saw a green roll of seaweed stretched along the white sandy beach. They gathered their arms full. Little sand fleas hopped wildly when the children touched the seaweed.

Mother scraped the fire coals away from the hot stones, then she and Father poured the clams into the hot pit. They covered them with piles of seaweed. Then on top they placed cat-tail mats. The seaweed and mats kept the heat inside. The water from the clams ran over the hot stones, making steam. The heat and steam opened the clam shells.

When Mother thought the clams were ready, she removed all the mats and seaweed and took the clams from the pit. Now she could easily slip the meat from the open shells and onto the ironwood drying sticks. When one stick was full, it was stuck into the ground near the fire which Father had burning. Then another stick was filled and so on until all the clams had been taken from the shells.

STEAMING AND CURING CLAMS AT SUMMER CAMPS

The drying sticks were tapered, larger at one end and gradually becoming smaller toward the other end. The clam meats were pushed over the sharp point and down toward the large end, which was forced into the ground. As the clams dried they could not slip off, nor down onto the ground.

The children stood close while their mother worked. As she emptied a shell they looked inside for bits of clam that might have been left. Sometimes they licked the good nectar from the shells.

Mother tended the fires and watched the sticks of drying clams, turning them to dry all sides. When they had partially dried, Mother slipped the clams from the sticks onto a length of twined nettle cord. She hung these strings of clams near the fire to finish drying. The strings of dried clams would later be put away in baskets up on the storage shelf inside their house at home.

With each low tide more clams were dug and put to dry until at last the Indians had enough for their winter food. Then they prepared still more to be used in trade with the Indians across the mountains. The inland Indians did not have salt water clams.

(25)

Mother saved all the largest clam shells for spoons and bowls.

After the clam drying was finished, the sticks were scraped and cleaned. They were saved for use another time.

One morning Mother called the children very early. "Today we travel back across the water to our home," she said. "We go out when the tide is high."

When the waves washed close to the canoes, the Indians were ready to leave. Father gave the signal to start. They were all glad to be going home. And the relatives at home would be happy to see them coming.

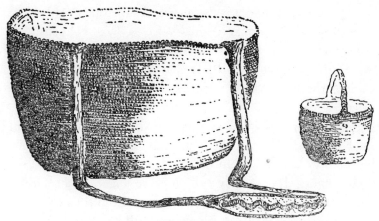

LARGE CEDAR ROOT BERRY BASKET WITH CARRYING STRAP
AND SMALL PICKING BASKET

Chapter VI

DAYS OF LEARNING

ONE DAY in the summer after the sun had warmed the earth, Mother said, "Children, today we will begin to gather blackberries."

The children danced around in glee. They loved the little blackberries that grew near the woods. Mother went inside the house to get the berry baskets. She gave one to Malitsa and one to Swaloos. The basket she kept was much larger. The berry baskets were tightly woven and each had a woven strip of cedar bark to fit over the shoulder.

They left the village and walked far up the shore. The big cedar trees grew farther apart here. Along the ground trailed prickly vines bearing juicy blackberries.

"Umm," said Swaloos and Malitsa and they began to pick the berries, eating them as fast as they picked.

Mother held up a warning hand. "No, no, my children, wait. Remember what Grandmother says."

The children did not remember and so Mother told them. Grandmother, Woman - Who - Weaves, was told by her grandmother that when children pick berries they must not eat until the basket is full. If they eat the berries first, the ends of the fingers will rot off and the basket will never be filled.

The children looked at the dark stains on the ends of their fingers. They looked at their empty baskets. They must hurry and fill them before the Great-Man should see their fingers. It was very bad to cause anger to the Great-Man, for He would turn His face away from them.

It seemed to take a long time to fill the baskets. They picked and picked. Finally Swaloos had his full. Then he helped his sister fill her basket.

"Now you may eat all the berries you want," Mother told them. "You have been very good children."

The two children began to eat berries from their baskets. Again Mother spoke to them, "No, no! You must pick the berries you eat."

Quickly they turned to look for berries on the vines. They picked and ate until they could eat no more. Then they took a nice ripe berry and painted lines on their faces. They wanted to look like the grownups who painted lines on their faces for ceremonials. Then they danced around in a circle, singing a little song.

While they rested from their dance, a little brown chipmunk scampered along a fallen tree trunk. The children saw the black stripes down his back. He stopped by a berry vine. He picked a berry, and sat up to eat it. He held the berry in his little front paws, and his bushy tail curled up against his back. The boy and girl sat very still so he would not be frightened away.

When Mother's basket was full and they carried their berries home, Mother spread the berries on a cedar bark mat in the sun to dry. Each day they gathered more berries and each day Mother would spread them on a mat, now and then stirring the berries around so the sun could draw all the moisture out. After the berries had dried well they were stored away in baskets for winter use.

One day when Mother was preparing a meal, she looked into the water bucket and found it empty.

"Swaloos," she called, "I would like to have some water."

Swaloos was playing with his bow and arrow, shooting at a mark on a tree. He frowned for he had not yet hit the mark and wanted to before he stopped shooting.

"I will shoot once more," he thought. He missed again and it made him angry. He threw down his bow and went to get the water.

WOODEN WATER BUCKETS AND WATER-TIGHT CARRYING BASKET
WITH HORN DIPPER

The water bucket was wooden. It was square with a small limb bent across for a handle. It was made of pieces of cedar boards hewed to the right thickness. The boards were put together with wooden pegs and the seams filled with pitch from the fir tree. Some buckets were hewed from a solid piece of wood. But Swaloos could not carry the heavy bucket full of water. He must use the water basket and make several trips to fill it. The men could carry the bucket full of water but the children could not.

Swaloos took the water basket and went to the creek. He dipped the basket into the fresh water and filled it. On the way back to the house, Swaloos was not careful how he carried the water. It sloshed as he walked and some of it spilled.

The Indian boy set the basket near his mother and started to run back to his play.

Mother looked into the basket. She saw it was only half full. "Oh, my son!" she called to Swaloos.

He stopped running and turned back to his mother. It is not good for the grandson of a chief to pretend he does not hear.

"My son," said Mother, "the basket is only half full. You remember what Grandfather said?"

The boy felt in his heart he must have done wrong. "I do not remember," he replied.

"Grandfather says," Mother told him, "then when the basket comes back not full it means the carrier is not good. It means he is not willing to do his work."

The boy hung his head. "That is right, Mother, I did not want to stop playing."

Mother shook her head sadly. She was ashamed of her boy.

Swaloos saw he had made his mother unhappy. "It will not happen again," he said. "I am sorry. Let me go back and do it over. I want to grow up to be a chief."

Swaloos ran to the creek and refilled the basket. This time he was very careful and when he set it down, it was full.

Malitsa was helping her mother with the meal. Mother had used a pestle and bowl to grind dried salmon eggs. Malitsa had been allowed to grind some, too. Then she had watched while Mother mixed the salmon eggs with flour.

"Where does the flour come from?" Malitsa asked.

Mother replied, "It comes from the fern root. Remember the day we gathered fern roots, way on the other side of the stream?"

She remembered that they had gone far away from the village to find the best fern roots and Mother had dug them with a digging stick.

Mother explained how she had prepared the fern roots to make the flour.

"I put them in the hot charcoals to bake. When they

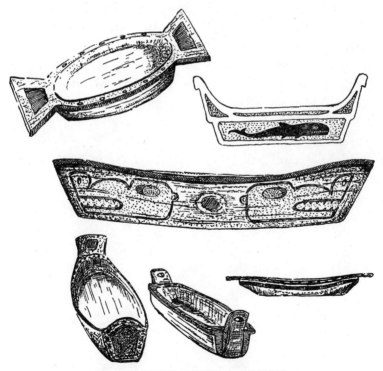

SERVING DISHES CARVED FROM WOOD

were done I held the roots over a flat stone and with a hard-wood stick beat the fern and scraped off the burned part. The inside was then beaten and pounded until it was powdered."

Malitsa knew the rest. She watched her mother mix the ground salmon eggs and flour with some water to make a dough. Mother took the dough in her clean hands and made it into little cakes. The cakes were put on a hot, flat stone beside the fire and left there to bake.

While the cakes baked Malitsa brought the dishes and eating mats. Most of these eating mats were woven from leaves of the cat-tail rush, but some were woven of cedar bark.

Malitsa liked to help set out the dishes. Most of them were nice white shells. The dishes she liked best were the platters and bowls carved from the wood of the maple tree. The bowls were shaped something like canoes, with designs painted on them. There were all sizes. Very small bowls were carved from wood or horn and were spoon shaped. The best ones had carvings on the handles. These were not all used for every day but were saved for special occasions.

Malitsa could hardly wait for the cakes to finish baking. She knew they would taste very good.

TOTEM STICK

Chapter VII

SURPRISES FOR THE CHILDREN

BOYS HAD TO LEARN to be very brave if they were to become great chiefs or brave warriors. Swaloos hoped to become a chief.

Very small boys were not allowed outside the house at night. When a boy began to grow up he was sent into the darkness to become brave.

One night Grandfather said to Swaloos, "Here, my little son, is the totem stick. I want you to take it all the way

(33)

around the house but do not bring it back. Leave it at the far corner of the house and I will get it in the morning."

Swaloos was excited. This meant his grandfather thought he was growing up. The totem stick was the family power stick. It was important and gave strength and power. To carry it one must have a clean body. The totem stick invited the guiding spirit to come close.

"Yes, Grandfather," Swaloos said, standing before his honored grandfather.

"Remember, he who is brave walks quietly and slowly," said Grandfather. "He never runs in the darkness. He listens to the night sounds. He thinks of the day he will become a great man."

"Yes, Grandfather," replied the boy.

"Now go, my little chief," Carver-of-Wood told him. "The spirits of our brave fathers will be near."

Swaloos lifted his chin and stood to his fullest height. He took the totem stick his grandfather handed to him and went out through the door into the darkness. He stood a moment looking about. It was not so dark after all. The round moon was moving along the tops of the trees.

Swaloos wondered which way he should go around the house. Grandfather had not said. For a moment he thought about it.

"I shall go around the woods side first," Swaloos said to himself. "The enemy comes by huge black canoes from across the water. When I come to the other end of the house I can see the water before I am seen. I can peek from behind the house and if the enemy is coming I can run back quickly along the woods side to warn my people."

Swaloos walked slowly, listening with eager ears. He heard many sounds among the trees. The little night animals were about. A "whooo" from a big tree startled Swaloos. He stopped for a moment, listening.

Then the boy smiled. "You can not frighten me, Mr. Owl,

up there in the tree. I know you." He did not speak aloud. He thought the words to himself. He went on again, moving cautiously.

When the boy came near the corner of the house he walked almost on tiptoe. He was trying very hard to be quiet. First he peeked carefully around the corner. Not seeing anyone he put his head around. He listened. His ears caught many sounds of the woods, but no sound of the enemy came to him.

Swaloos walked cautiously along the side of the house. At the other corner he could see across the water. He pressed flat against the house while he watched and listened. No dip of a paddle disturbed the lap, lap of the waves. When Swaloos was sure no one was about, he placed the totem stick on a log, then started on. He walked along the water side of the long house, still being very quiet. He paused once more to listen before entering the door. Then he went inside. He was proud. Grandfather saw by his face that he had been a brave boy.

Malitsa was not allowed to go outside the house at night. Only the boys and men went out alone. While Swaloos was learning to be brave, Malitsa was learning things too. She was learning to be like her mother.

After Swaloos had gone outside that evening, Grandfather said, "Come, young daughter, I have a present for you."

Malitsa rose from the bench to go to her grandfather. She was very careful not to walk between her grandfather and the fire. She had already learned that was not polite. She must go around behind the grown people. The Indian girl walked softly with her head held high, her body straight.

"Yes, Grandfather," Malitsa said, standing before Grandfather.

The old man reached behind him and brought out a little

baby board. Strapped on the board was a doll carved from wood.

"Oh, oh," exclaimed Malitsa, her eyes shining. "A new doll and a baby board for it." She reached her arms for the wonderful new toy.

"You are to learn some of the care of a baby, little daughter," the old Chief told her.

"Oh, Grandfather, I am learning," she said proudly. "I go often to the house of Swinging-Fringes to help her with the baby."

"That is fine, my child," Grandfather said.

"Thank you so much for the beautiful gift," said the girl. "I am very happy." And her eyes showed her happiness.

Grandfather was pleased. He nodded and Malitsa went back to her seat. She did not skip nor run, but walked softly and carefully. Children must not run inside the house.

Malitsa was smiling happily as she examined her baby board. It was just like the real board Swinging-Fringes had for her baby.

Mother took some shredded cedar bark from her work basket, and said, "You may have this to pad your board."

She thanked her mother, then she put some of the soft bark on the board. She made a little pad for the doll's neck. And another to fit the back, just as she had watched Swinging-Fringes do. The pads were to fit the board to the baby's body, to make him comfortable.

Malitsa put her doll on the board. She was careful how she placed it. Then she folded the blanket just so and drew the straps around the doll. They must not be too tight, she remembered. Nor too loose.

The Indian mother watched. When Malitsa had finished she showed it to her mother. Mother smiled. "You have done well, my little daughter."

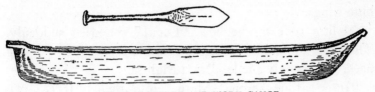

WOMAN'S PADDLE AND WORK CANOE

Chapter VIII

GATHERING CAT-TAIL RUSHES

THE SUMMER DAYS were warm and long. The Indians worked very hard preparing for the coming winter. Malitsa and Swaloos were a great help to their mother.

One day Grandmother said to Mother, "We need more cat-tail mats. Some are wearing out. And the children are growing taller. It would be well to gather fresh rushes."

"I will gather a new supply," Mother said. And early the next morning she called the children from their play. "We are going to gather cat-tails," she told them.

"May I carry your paddle?" Swaloos asked.

"Yes, son. You may also paddle the canoe for me," Mother said. Swaloos was glad. His mother's canoe was not like the canoes of the men but the boy liked to paddle it. The paddle was different, too. The women had their own paddles and canoes, shaped differently from those of the men. Swaloos did not care. He could paddle his mother's canoe and pretend he was a great warrior. He tried to paddle as quietly as possible. The enemy might be somewhere near. He was always on the look-out for the enemy.

Swaloos guided the small canoe along close to shore until he came to a slough which emptied into the salt water. Mother told Swaloos to turn and follow up the slough. The dugout made a little ripple ahead of it as it slipped through

(37)

the quiet water. Dragonflies darted about on their fragile blue wings.

Malitsa rode in the bow. "Look!" she cried suddenly. They saw a strange looking bird with a long bill and a long neck. "It has only one leg," said Malitsa.

"It is a blue heron," Mother told them. "It has two very long legs. The other is folded up under it. Watch when it flies and you will see. The heron is watching for fish."

Just then the big bird flapped its huge wings and rose from the slough. Drops of water dripped from two long legs as the heron flew up and away.

Around a bend in the slough they saw the cat-tails. Cat-tails are very like large grass. They were taller than Mother's head. The slender, blade-like leaves swayed and quivered in the breeze. Swaloos pushed the canoe in among the stalks while his mother gathered the long green leaves. Malitsa placed the leaves in the canoe as her mother handed them to her. They must be placed carefully for Mother wanted to take a big load of them home.

They worked long. When the sun was directly overhead, Mother gave each child a piece of dried venison, and had one for herself. They chewed the good dry meat and liked the smoky flavor. Then they went to work again.

The sun was big and red down close to the ocean when the Indians turned their canoe homeward. The pile of cat-tails was tied across with nettle cord, for Mother did not want to lose any from the pile. The canoe did not paddle as easily as before it was loaded. Mother took her extra paddle and helped Swaloos.

Soon they saw the fires of their village. It was near meal time. Many fires burned brightly.

Father came to help them unload the rushes. They all carried some to a chosen spot and there the leaves were spread out to sun-dry and cure. In the next few days Mother would watch them and turn them each day. The sun would change their color from green to light brown. The leaves must dry just right to wear well. Then they would be put away for winter weaving.

"Come!" called Grandmother. "I have prepared the meal."

The children hurried for they were very hungry.

Father had caught a sockeye salmon while Mother and the children were away gathering cat-tails. Grandmother tended sticks of salmon leaning toward the fire. The crusty red squares smelled extra good.

COOKING SALMON ON STICKS

The children ran to wash their hands and were back in no time. Mother and Father came, too. All were very hungry. Mother wanted to help Grandmother serve the meal.

"You rest, my daughter," said the old mother. "You have worked hard and long."

"Yes, I am tired," the young mother replied. "For many,

many days we have prepared for winter. A rest would be welcome."

"You shall rest," Grandmother told her. "It is not yet time to go to the mountains to hunt. I will prepare the meals and tend the home for you."

The young mother was glad.

The evening meal was now ready for the hungry family but before they started to eat they all raised a hand to give thanks for their food. This was important. If they did not show their thankfulness a great time of hunger might come to their people.

The children started to eat very fast. Grandmother watched while bite after bite was swallowed. Then she said, "Children, you are not chewing well."

"We are so hungry," said Malitsa.

"I remember what my grandmother told me," said their grandmother.

Swaloos and Malitsa stopped eating to listen. It was very impolite to eat while being spoken to. Besides, they always liked to hear what the old people had said. That was how the young Indians learned of the times gone by.

"Once I was eating very fast, and not chewing," said the old lady. "My kind old grandmother told me the food was going down saying, 'Hurrah, hurrah, I am only lightly chewed.' She said the food was laughing at me. The food knew that later it would cause trouble inside me. Then I would have bad dreams."

The old lady went on with her story while the children listened. "My grandmother was old and wise and I knew I must do as she said. I chewed very hard, I was not going to let the food be stronger than I. I chewed so the food would not jump around inside me when I tried to go to sleep. It could not cause me any trouble."

Swaloos and Malitsa thought about the story their grandmother had just told them. She must be right. For now she was old and no longer a little girl as when her grandmother had told her the story. The children chewed their food well, and did not eat so fast. They wanted to be sure it was not saying to them, 'Hurrah, hurrah, I am only lightly chewed."

Chapter IX

LOOKING FORWARD TO A JOURNEY

SWALOOS LAY ON THE BEACH in the summer sun. His brown skin glistened with drops of salt water. He had been swimming.

"Come on!" someone shouted. "Blackfish and Seal!"

Swaloos sprang up and ran to the water. Other boys ran into the water, too, and they all began to swim about. "Blackfish and Seal" was a game they played. Some of the boys would be seals and others blackfish. The seals swam ahead, and the blackfish chased them.

Soon all the Indian boys were diving under and coming up again, as blackfish and seals swim.

"Swim fast and duck," called Swaloos to his seal friends. Away they went, splashing and cutting the water.

One small boy was afraid. When he saw the blackfish after him he swam for the shore and ran out.

The big boys jeered at him. But the girls, who had gathered along the shore to cheer and shout warnings to the players, were sorry for the little fellow.

"We would be afraid too," Malitsa told him. "Those boys are big."

"But you are a girl," said the small one. "Boys are supposed to be brave, and girls are not. I am ashamed."

"Do not feel badly," comforted Malitsa. "When you are older you will be one of the blackfish, I am sure."

A loud shout rang from the water. The blackfish had caught all the seals. They were bringing them to shore. The boys came out, laughing and blowing water. They dropped down on the warm sand, panting from their hard swim. The sun dried the salt water on their strong young bodies while they rested and talked.

"When the sun sleeps and comes again, we shall travel," said one of the boys.

"Ah," Swaloos sighed, "I am very happy. I have never traveled so far. This time my father says I may go."

"I am going, too," said Swaloos' friend, Jumping-Boy. "We shall have a good time together. We shall see many new things."

"Yes, that is so," agreed Swaloos.

"And we shall hunt with the men," Jumping-Boy said, feeling very grownup.

"The men are very particular. They may not let us go. My father says small boys frighten the deer and other animals," Swaloos told his friend.

"I can be as quiet as the men," Jumping-Boy boasted.

"I can, too," said Swaloos, "only my father does not think so. If he will give me a chance I will show him how grownup I can be."

Mother came out of the house and called Swaloos. He went running quickly. Boys must always obey their parents immediately, Swaloos had been taught. It is not manly to frown and walk slowly when one is called.

Mother said to her son, "We travel when the sun comes up from behind the mountains. Grandmother and Grandfather will not go. They are too old. It would be very kind of you to gather wood for them before we leave."

Malitsa came up to the house while Mother was speaking. "It would be kind of Malitsa to help, too," Mother added.

"Of course I will help," said Malitsa.

"And I will help," said Jumping-Boy, "because I have no old people who will be left behind."

Swaloos and Malitsa were sorry for Jumping-Boy. It was nice having old people in one's house. The Indians considered it an honor and very lucky to have old relatives with them. The children were taught to honor and respect all old people. They were taught to be kind and to help whenever possible.

"Every kindness to the aged," their parents had told them, "will come back to you many times greater, even though years later."

The children went to work. They sang as they carried many armloads of wood. They made a pile near the house.

Grandmother and Grandfather were very pleased. When the children had finished the old ones called to them.

"Come, children, we want to thank you."

The children smiled. They were very happy because they had helped the old ones.

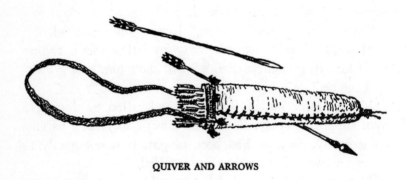

QUIVER AND ARROWS

Grandfather gave each boy a quiver for his arrows.

"Oh," the boys cried together, "it is just like father's." They looked at each other and laughed. Had they not had the same thought?

Grandmother gave Malitsa a small buckskin bag. It was stained with red dust. "Bring back some color dust from the mountains," she told Malitsa, "and I will show you how to use it."

The girl was very pleased. This meant Grandmother thought she was growing up. Grandmother was going to show her how to beautify her face.

Chapter X

MOVING UP-RIVER

THE NEXT DAY Swaloos and Malitsa were up before the sun.

Grandfather had rapped on the wall with his stick to waken the household.

Blue smoke curled up into the air from many roused fires. Other families of the village were going to start for the mountains to hunt, also.

Grandmother ground dry fish for the morning meal. Mother packed bedding mats, food, baskets, and all the other things they would need. The children helped. Father loaded the traveling canoe.

As soon as breakfast had been eaten, the Indians prepared to leave. Mother brought the red paint for their faces. Always the Indians painted their faces before starting on a journey for the grease paint protected their skins from sun and wind.

At last they were ready. The old people went down to the water's edge with them. As the loaded canoes pulled out from the shore, the old people sang a farewell song. The song wished a safe and profitable journey. Their arms waved in rhythm. When the song no longer reached across the water to the canoes, Father stood up and raised his arm skyward in farewell to the old ones left behind.

Many paddles dipped and pushed the canoes along. The children wanted to go faster. The fathers knew that harder paddling would come soon enough, so they saved their strength.

The canoes moved steadily on. The clear green salt water had become clouded and no longer could the children see deep into the water.

"We are coming to the mouth of the river," said Father. "The river water is muddy as it flows into the bay. Melting snows rush down creeks to the river. Then the swiftly moving water gathers sand and silt on the downward run to the sea."

Father turned his canoe, changing its course into the broad spread of the river mouth. One by one the other canoes swung up the river. The men changed their paddles for long, slim poles. They must stand in their canoes, now, and urge them upstream by bracing their poles on the river bottom and pushing hard against them.

The children noticed the movement of the water. It no longer had the scooping rhythm of the salt waves. The muddy light green water moved onward and onward, sometimes circling into small eddies, at other times swinging around a sand bar. But always the river urged its quietly swirling waters on to the sea. It was not easy for Father to work the canoe up-stream against the current.

The sun hung high. Mother gave the children and Father strips of dried salmon. The children were hungry and chewed with delight. Father was hungry from his hard work. Mother had helped with the poling and she, too, chewed a strip of salmon. They saw the Indians in the other canoes were also eating.

Soon the river was not so wide as it had been at the mouth. The water flowed more swiftly. Bushy green trees grew close along the banks. A cedar tree leaned far out over the river and some of its branches tripped in the water. The Indians saw where the never ceasing flow of the water had eaten the soil away from the roots on one side. Father stooped while the canoe slipped under the slanting tree.

Long green shadows darkened the water as the sun slowly settled down behind the far away islands. Before dusk the Indians reached a camping ground. In a bend of the river a sand bar jutted out. Father signaled to his tribesmen. The

Indians hauled their canoes up on the sandy beach.

"Children," said Mother, "you may gather twigs and wood for the fire while I unload the sleeping mats and food from the canoe."

The children were glad to run about gathering dry wood. They had been still in the canoe for so long it was good to be out.

SWALOOS TRYING TO START A FIRE

"May I start the fire?" Swaloos asked his mother.

"You are very young, my son, but you may try," Mother replied.

The boy was so excited he wanted to jump and shout, but he remembered a well behaved young man does not do such things.

Mother brought the fire material from the canoe. She carried it in a special bag made of cedar bark. To make the bag, a length of green or raw cedar bark had been bent into the desired size, left to season and dry into shape. The sides were laced with thong, and a shoulder strap fastened on.

Mother took from the bag some finely shredded cedar bark, a piece of pitch wood, and a short board in which a small hole had been drilled. Kneeling, she placed the material near the dry twigs the children had gathered.

"Here, my young man," said Mother, handing a short pointed cottonwood stick to Swaloos.

Swaloos took the stick, his heart pounding in excitement. He knelt with his knee on one end of the board to steady it. He placed the point of the stick into the hole and tucked the tinder close around it. Swaloos held the stick between his palms, rubbing them back and forth. Faster and faster whirled the stick. The boy watched the tinder anxiously, but no smoke appeared. He tried to whirl the stick faster. Still no smoke. A lump crowded up in his throat. He swallowed it back. The grandson of a chief may feel disappointment but he does not cry.

"I shall wait a little longer, Mother," the boy said.

Mother took the stick, smiling at her son. "Only a little longer, my boy."

The stick spun expertly in the mother's strong hands. A thread of smoke coiled upward from the shredded cedar bark. Quickly Mother gathered the smouldering tinder in her cupped hands and gently blew on it. From a tiny spark, a young flame grew, and spread through the tinder. Mother hurriedly placed the growing fire on the ground, carefully adding splinters of pitch wood and twigs. Spitting and popping, the small puffs of black smoke rolled up from the burning pitch. Soon the fire was blazing brightly.

An evening meal of dried clams was prepared and the Indians ate heartily.

After the meal was over, Mother chose a place to make their beds. She moved aside a few rocks and broken limbs. Then the cat-tail sleeping mats were spread on the dry sand, beneath over-hanging bushes. The Indians did not put up a shelter this night, for on the morrow they would continue their journey up the river.

The children went to sleep with the song of the river in their ears. The night sounds here were different.

Swaloos had been asleep for some time when he heard a strange sound. He listened without moving. He thought he might still be asleep but he knew by the pounding of his heart that something had startled him from his sleep. His ears told him it was the sound of an animal. Its heavily ambling feet overturned pebbles as it splashed along the water's edge. Swaloos raised up on his elbow and looked. A bear! The bear seemed huge and dark in the silvery light from the moon. The boy watched it swing its big body as it walked.

Slowly the bear raised its nose, and with hunting sniffs picked up the scent of food. It shuffled toward the canoes.

"Our food," thought Swaloos, "the bear will get our food." He sat up quickly and spoke to his father. The bear whirled at the sound, rearing to its haunches. It had not yet caught the human scent. Then with a snorting blow from its nose, the bear plunged into the water and crossed the river, crashing into the woods on the other side. Father had jumped up with his weapons but he was too late.

"The bear was going for our food," cried Swaloos excitedly.

"My son," said Father quietly, "a good hunter never moves quickly nor speaks loudly."

Shame spread over the boy. He felt like hiding under his covers. He knew now that he should have spoken very quietly.

"I am not worthy of being the son of a great hunter," the young voice spoke humbly.

Father kneeled and reached a kindly hand for the small drooping shoulders. "You were a good boy to think of our food," he said. "I am sure you will remember to be quiet next time."

Swaloos felt better but his cheeks burned with the thoughts of his carelessness. He fell asleep thinking of the lesson he had just learned.

Chapter XI

FARTHER ALONG THE RIVER TRAIL

Streaks of color were brightening the sky the next morning when the Indians climbed into their canoes to continue up the water trail. The children were anxious to be on their way.

Quietly the canoes, one behind another, nosed up-river. There was very little talking among the Indians. The children watched the banks for animals.

Suddenly a noisy flapping of wings tore at the leaves of a tall cottonwood tree, high above the travelers. A great dark bird with a shining white head soared across the opening above the river. Back and forth, and around it circled.

"The mighty eagle is looking for fish," Father explained. "It was hidden in one of the cottonwoods."

Father fitted an arrow against the bowstring. The big bird soared over once more, but Father stopped its flight with a well aimed arrow. The others halted their canoes while Father brought back his game. Its beautiful eagle feathers would be very useful, and the sharp, curved claws would make fine decorations for clothes.

The line of canoes moved on, slowly, push by push. When the sun's last rays had left the treetops, the Indians made their second night camp.

Again in the morning, the travelers poled their cedar dugouts upstream. The water became swift. Poling was hard work. Father must be careful not to let the current turn the canoe and carry it back downstream. Mother helped with her pole.

Above the whispering sweep of the river Swaloos could hear a dull roar. He listened. Malitsa heard it, too. Father saw them listening, and said, "It is the big waterfall. Beyond the bend, you will see the river falling over a cliff."

The children watched anxiously. Louder grew the noise until it was frightening, as if something big were about to rush down upon them. And then they saw above them a great curtain of silvery water pouring down from high rocks. It splashed and danced below the cliff, then smoothed out to flow swiftly onward, down toward them.

"Oh, look!" breathed Malitsa in excitement. A great elk lifted his head, water dripping from his mouth. He gazed for a startled second, then turned and broke into the woods.

"He had come to drink at the pool below the falls," Father explained. "He did not hear us in the noise of the waterfall for our scent was blowing downstream, away from the animal. Hunters are always careful that the wind carries the human scent away from, not toward the animal."

Swaloos thought to himself, "I will remember what my father says. Someday I shall be a great hunter. I must remember to notice which way the wind blows."

But another thought came to him quickly as he looked at the high waterfall. "How will we get over it?" he asked Father.

"We go around," Father answered. He gave the signal and turned his canoe to the sandy bank. One by one those following pulled up beside the leader. The children sat quietly until Father gave the word to get out. But Jumping-Boy had already hopped out of his father's canoe.

"What are we going to do?" he asked the leader's children.

Swaloos knew it was not right for Jumping-Boy to move before the command was given, and he hesitated before answering. Finally, he replied, "My father says we go around."

Mother was close by and heard the children talking. "We unload and carry everything around through the woods to get beyond the falls," she explained to them. "Then we again load the canoes and go on up the river."

The children watched while Mother prepared the packs. She rolled the mats and tied them with nettle cord packing straps. She made small packs for the children. Each must do his share of the work. They raised the packs to their backs, and adjusted the straps across their foreheads.

Father led the way with the first load, Mother and the children following him through the woods. The man always walked ahead. They climbed up, through brush and between big trees. The first loads of the relay were piled on the river bank above the falls and the Indians went back for more.

Others were coming up behind them. They followed the trail the leader had made through the brush. Baskets of food were fastened to the packing straps and balanced upon the toughened brown backs. The women and children would finish alone now, for the men must help one another with the canoes. The dugouts were heavy and it took the strength of many men to move them.

After much hard struggling the last canoe had been brought up. It would soon be ready with the others.

Father was thirsty. At the water's edge, upstream from the waiting canoes, he lay flat and filled his mouth with cold water. But he did not drink it. He stood up, turned his back to the river, and from his mouth he blew water in a spray over the green foliage about him. Then he again lay down beside the river and took water into his mouth. This time he drank.

Malitsa and Swaloos had watched their father. "He is thanking the Great-Man who created all the people," said the boy to his sister. "Our father says we must always spray the water to share with other living things. It would be selfish to drink without first giving water to the little growing plants."

Other men came to drink also. Each of them sprayed water as Father had done.

They all rested and chewed smoked salmon. Then Father gave the signal to be on their way. The children were very quiet, climbing into their places. The mothers were already in the bows waiting to help with their poles. Father took his pole and pushed the canoe from the bank, again pointing its bow upstream. The others followed in order. The water was smooth and not so swift, and poling was not as hard as it had been below the falls.

When the sun told the travelers the day had grown old, they made their night camp in a grove of alder trees. Swaloos and his friend Jumping-Boy scouted around the camp site. On one side they found a slough backed in from the river, and its still brown water looked threatening to the boys.

"I do not like that dark water," said Jumping-Boy, backing away from the slough bank.

"Neither do I," agreed Swaloos, "it is too still, as if it might be hiding evil beneath the smoothness. See, there is not a ripple except the little skipper bugs darting about. Let us go."

The boys circled the camp site and came to a small stream. The gay water bubbled and sommersaulted among rocks, making the boys feel light-hearted and eager again.

They followed up its course as it wound among the old and young alders.

"Why, look!" whispered Swaloos, pointing ahead. "Someone lives here."

"And they have been cutting down trees," added Jumping-Boy.

Cautiously the boys moved ahead. They saw many trees cut down across the creek, and brush piled among the felled trees. They listened, ears straining for the sound of the workers. But not a sound came to them. They crept on, watching, careful not to step on a twig. They had reached the heaviest pile of brush when Swaloos grasped Jumping-Boy's arm, whispering softly, "It is a dam. See the mud and limbs matted together? Listen."

The boys held their breath, listening intently. The sound of gnawing reached their ears. Their eyes searched eagerly for the source of the sound. Suddenly a little brown animal came from behind a tree not far from them. He began to gnaw. The boys saw a gnawed ring around the tree where the animal was working.

BEAVERS AT WORK

"I know," whispered Swaloos, "it is a beaver. Father told me how they cut down trees and build dams."

"So it is," Jumping-Boy whispered back, almost hopping in his excitement.

The little animal was intent on his work and did not hear the boys. Light was fading and the boys knew they

(54)

must return to camp. The beaver stopped work, walked over to the stream and disappeared under the water.

"His home is down in the dam," said Swaloos. "I wish we could see it."

"Do you suppose we could find it by digging in?" suggested Jumping-Boy.

"Oh, no, that would be mean," cried Swaloos. "Then the beaver would have to move away and build a new home. Come, we must go back to camp. Darkness is drawing close."

They hurried back to the others to tell of their adventure.

Chapter XII

THE TEMPORARY CAMP

DAY AFTER DAY the string of cedar dugouts followed the course of the water trail to the mountains.

The travelers were now anxious to reach the end of their journey. The children looked ahead, eagerly. A warm rosy glow from the late afternoon sun painted the tall evergreens. Up the river's slash through the timber, the mountains loomed large and grand.

Malitsa sighed. "It is more beautiful than I dreamed," she said softly.

"Ah," Swaloos breathed, expanding his chest and lifting his face toward the mountains.

Mother and Father stopped their poles to lift their faces to the mountains, in prayer. They all felt small beneath the towering masses of aged ice and rock.

The poles were at work again, finding a solid bottom to force the canoes ahead. Timbered banks gave way to a wide sand bar and Father signaled that they had at last come to their temporary camp site. The canoe grated against the sand as Father ran it aground.

The Indians hustled about, choosing their camping places. Each family must have a sleeping shelter and a place to cook and eat. Malitsa went with her mother, and watched.

"See," Mother told her, "we choose a level spot on higher ground for the beds. If rain comes, the water drains into the low places. The higher ground does not become so wet."

"I will remember," the girl replied.

"The Mighty-One may send rain at any time. Our people must always be prepared," Mother explained. "Over here, we will have our fire. We do not build a fire close to trees

TEMPORARY CAT-TAIL MAT SHELTER AT SUMMER CAMP

for the red tongues of the fire are greedy. They might run away from us and destroy many growing things, birds and animals, too. The Great-Man would be angry and sorrow might come to our people."

Malitsa thought how terrible it would be to see fire running through the forest, burning everything. She shuddered.

"The canoes must be unloaded," Mother told the children. And they all went to bring poles and mats and thongs to erect their shelter.

Mother stood two crotched poles three strides apart, asking the children each to hold one. Then she laid a third pole across between the two, tying them together with a cedar root thong. This was the front of their shelter frame. Beside each crotch she placed one end of another set of poles, slanting them back to rest on the ground. She made the upper ends secure to the crotches. The slanting poles had notches about arm's length apart and Mother laid cross poles to support the roof. Over the frame work she spread the cat-tail shelter mats, overlapped to shed water in case of rain. She pinned them with cedar pins, so they would stay in place.

After the mats were all in place, Mother showed the children how to make the shelter warmer inside, for the mountain air was cold. She held the lower ends of the mats down and scooped sand up over the edges. She found some rocks and carefully laid them on the sand. This would keep the little ground breezes from blowing under the mats.

Now Mother and Malitsa took the bedding mats inside the shelter and spread them on the ground to make their beds. Blankets woven from mountain goat wool, duck down and cedar thread were used, too.

The shelter and beds were ready. Malitsa was happy for she felt she had learned a great deal. It made her feel very grown up.

"Wood for the fire!" called Mother.

Malitsa looked around for her brother. She saw him coming, running from the up-river direction.

"Mother needs wood for the supper fire," Malitsa told him.

Swaloos was breathless. "Do you hear that roar?" he panted, as the two went to find wood.

"Yes," Malitsa replied. "Is it another waterfall?"

"No," her brother said. "It is river spirits howling in a gorge."

The girl's eyes grew large with excitement.

"River spirits?"

"Yes, there are two high rock cliffs close together and the river squeezes between them," the boy exclaimed. "I saw it. The water piles up and rushes through. Then it turns round and round into a dark green whirlpool. And old tree snags jump up and down and roll in it. Father says it is very deep and angry. We must not go near it."

"Oh, I would be afraid of it," said Malitsa.

"And Father says our people never take their canoes through that water. The angry spirits would dash a canoe to pieces. It is cruel and wild. The cliffs crush the spirit of the river as it is squeezed between them and it screams and makes an awful noise. Its anger is spent in the whirling and boiling of the green pool. From there it flows on as a quiet river."

"I am afraid," shuddered Malitsa. "Let us gather our wood and hurry."

"There is no reason to be afraid," her brother said, "but we must go back to camp."

They each carried an armful of wood to their mother. It was good to be with the grown people near the friendly fires.

Smoke from new camp fires curled into the evening air and drifted downstream with the river.

Chapter XIII

THE HUNTERS

BUSY DAYS LAY AHEAD of the Indians at their temporary camp in the mountains. They were out of their sleeping mats very early.

"I wish I could go with the men," sighed Swaloos as he watched them prepare for the hunt.

"Some day you will be old enough to go. It might be very soon," said Father. "We shall see."

The boy felt better. Maybe it would not be so long after all.

ARROWS — BONE AND STONE TIPS

"You may hold the quiver," Father told him. Swaloos was pleased. He looked at the tanned hide quiver with the fur turned inside. It was made just like the smaller one his grandfather had given him. He watched his father. Very carefully Father examined each of his arrows. He tried the strength of the slender cedar shafts to make sure they were not split. He looked at the points of bone and stone. One by one the arrows were replaced in the quiver. Father tested his bow, and was satisfied with it.

"You are wearing different clothes, Father," observed

Swaloos, studying the rough elk skin shirt and long trouser-like leggings his father wore.

"Yes," Father replied, "I wear these for hunting. Sometimes the bushes between the big trees are cruel. The weight of heavy snows has caused them to grow tough and sharp. Their pointed fingers tear at the skin."

"Will I wear such clothes when I am allowed to hunt?" asked Swaloos.

"Yes," Father answered. "Mother will make them for you. She will weave the belt from cedar bark and wool. I will show you how to wrap the long belt around your waist to hold the trousers in place."

Swaloos saw that some of the men wore long trousers woven from beaten cedar bark, and they had cedar bark leggings below the knee. The inner bark had been used while it was still green. It was cut the right size and shaped around the legs and bound. It was left to dry in the form of the leg so it would hold that shape. Such leggings would wear well.

"It is so long to wait to become a man," sighed Swaloos.

His father smiled. "Many years ago it seemed long to me, my son, but the time passes quickly while you learn. It is not long now for you to wait." He placed a strong hand on his boy's shoulder. "You stay by Mother for a few more seasons, then you will take your place with the men."

Father tucked the knife made of mussel shell into his belt and signaled to his friends. The men, carrying bows, with quivers slung over their shoulders, followed. Their leader led the way toward the high mountains beyond the trees. Swaloos watched how proudly his father walked. When the men had disappeared, the little boy straightened his shoulders and tried walking just as his father had.

Swaloos saw his mother watching him. He felt shy. Then he saw by the smile in her eyes that she was proud of him, too.

"While Father is hunting," Mother told the children, "we shall gather blueberries and mountain grasses."

Mother brought the berry baskets with straps attached. They were stained from much use. Mother and some women relatives with their children, took their baskets and crossed to the evergreen woods. The trees were so large and close together the path was shaded and cool. The moss felt soft underfoot. The way was very steep and the Indians had to dig their toes into the soft earth. Up and up they climbed, the children puffing with short breaths, and the mothers stopping to rest now and then.

Shafts of brighter light showed between the trees. Soon they were out of the dense timber and in thickets of alder saplings. The saplings were curved downhill, with their tops straining back toward the sun. This made travel very difficult and the children complained.

"Why do they grow so?" they wanted to know.

"The weight of the deep winter snow presses down upon them until they can no longer resist. They grow as they are bent. Only a little way now and we will be out of the alders," Mother said.

Suddenly there were no more alder saplings to fight against. There before them, seeming almost close enough to touch, the giant mountain stood. Awed, the children looked at the masses of gray-blue stone. It was rough, as if a mighty hand had chiseled carelessly, then filled and smoothed some places with snow and green ice.

Stretching across the meadows, from their feet toward the mountain, the ground was a patchwork of dark green heather, red leaves of low blueberry bushes, and yellowing grass.

They all set to work picking berries to fill their baskets. The children remembered the story their mother had told them, that their fingers would drop off if they ate the berries before their baskets were full. This time they did not eat until their little baskets were heaped with blueberries. Then how good the berries tasted to the hungry workers.

The sun had passed its high point in the sky and the time had come to go down to their river camp.

It was fun going down the steep hillside among the trees. The children had to dig in their heels to keep from pitching forward on their noses. And, too, they must be careful not to spill their berries. In no time at all they could see their camp.

Mother set to work. She was spreading the berries on a brown cedar bark mat to dry when Father came out of the woods and hailed them. He and his men brought loads of fresh elk meat. They were pleased with the first day's hunt.

There was hustle about the camp fires. Mother and the other women fanned their fires immediately. They called to the children to bring wood.

While the fires gained heat, the women brought sticks of ironwood. They cut the fresh meat into pieces and forced them on the sticks. They pushed one end of each stick into the ground near the fire, slanting the stick so the pieces would sizzle and brown. Soon the good smell of browning meat filled the air. Supper would be festive in honor of the first game of the hunt.

But while the fires burned and the meat was being prepared, Swaloos had decided to go hunting. He was only pretending, he told himself, though he followed the way of the returned hunters. He carried his bow, and slung across his shoulder were his play arrows in the quiver his grandfather had given him. Swaloos walked proudly as a brave hunter. He did not go far until he turned from the path and went among the big trees.

It was time for the evening meal and Swaloos had not yet returned. Evening shadows were settling down upon the camp. Mother became worried when Swaloos did not answer her bird call. He knew the call well for Mother had used it all his life. Father watched and listened. He knew these woods were not familiar to Swaloos.

"I shall go and find our boy," said Father.

Very carefully he examined the trail leading toward the

COUGAR

mountain. Yes, there were small footprints now and then. Sometimes the prints were not easily found as Father searched along the trail. He looked for bent grass blades or scuffed leaves. He examined the moss to see if the weight of a foot had pressed it down. In the moss he found the place where Swaloos had left the trail.

Father could follow more easily now for there were no other footprints to confuse him. The dents of small moccasins were plain in the deep moss. Father noticed that each print showed the boy had been careful not to step on twigs, and it pleased him. He had told Swaloos that the great hunter does not allow a twig to snap under his feet.

The trail of small footprints wound in and out among giant evergreens. Father followed, eyes and ears alert to every sign. Dusk was beginning to cast gloomy shadows. Father hurried. Suddenly the man was aware of a hushed feeling about him. It was as though even the big trees held their breath. He stood still and listened, his eyes searching. There was not a sound yet something warned him of danger. He moved on, stealthily, his bow and arrow poised, ready.

Slowly Father stepped from behind a huge fir tree. There stood Swaloos, his feet spread apart, holding his small bow and arrow in careful aim. Father looked up in the direction the arrow pointed. There, crouching on a leaning tree, a cougar watch Swaloos. His greedy eyes glittered in the half light. The big cat made no movement, except that the tip of his tail was twitching nervously. He was about to spring.

Swaloos had not heard his father's approach. He held the taut bow string with a steady hand. Then he let go. At the same instant a mightier bow string twanged and a mightier arrow sang through the air. With a scream, the big cat leaped toward its prey but the long tawny body fell short. The shaft of a large arrow quivered and was still. Beside it hung a small arrow. It, too, had hit its mark.

Swaloos saw the larger arrow in the cat's body. He

(65)

turned to find his father smiling at him. His eyes were round with surprise.

"Ah, my son," said Father, proudly, "you are brave. You will become a great hunter. But remember, the giant cat is cunning. You have done well." The boy smiled happily.

Together the two hunters went back to camp. Across Father's shoulders rested the huge cat still bearing the two arrows. Others at the camp must see the good omen for the hunter's son. Swaloos followed behind his father, carrying both bows and quivers. He did not notice when Father's quiver swayed against his knee, nor that the long bow tip sometimes dragged against the ground. Father and son were the same, two hunters, one looking back to his boyhood, the other looking forward to manhood.

That night there was a special fire and dancing to honor Swaloos.

DRYING RACKS

Chapter XIV

HARVESTING BASKET GRASSES

MALITSA WAS UP EARLY to help her mother prepare the elk meat for drying. She wanted to learn because it was the work of a woman.

Mother laid out the meat which had not been cooked for the evening meal. With a sharp mussel shell knife she cut it into strips the right size for drying. Then she set up the drying racks by driving small poles into the ground and laying other small poles across between the crotches. The strips of elk were hung from the cross poles over the fire so the smoke and gentle heat could dry it.

"See," said Mother, showing her daughter, "the fire does not blaze high. It does not need to be too hot. But there must be plenty of smoke. The smoke also keeps away insects

(67)

from the meat. The fire must be kept alive for days until the meat is dry."

The fat parts of the elk had been cut separately and these Mother arranged on a special smaller rack. Under each piece she placed a clam shell to catch every drop of the melted fat. This elk fat which is called tallow would be saved to prepare face paint. Some would be used for the women and girls to beautify the skin.

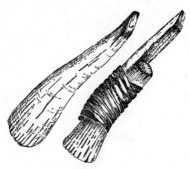

ELK HORN AND STONE CHISEL
ELK HORN CHISEL

Most of the elk was used for some particular need of the Indians. The hide was tanned to make bed covers. They removed the hair from a skin when it was to be used for clothing. The horns were saved for chisels and wedges; the bones for tools, awls, fish spears and arrow points, or for decorations. Even the hoofs were saved to be strung for ceremonials.

When the elk had all been taken care of, Mother and Malitsa went to tend their drying berries. The berries had been spread out on cedar bark mats woven of strips two fingers wide, and placed in the hottest sun. The girl watched her mother move the berries about on the mat so the under sides would be turned up to the hot sun.

"The sun draws the moisture out of the berries," Mother explained. "They will not spoil if thoroughly dry. After they have dried we will put them away in baskets for winter."

"I like berries," Malitsa said. "I want to gather more of them."

"Berries are very good food," Mother told her. "We will gather as many as we can. We must also gather grasses for baskets. Grandmother will be sad if we do not bring plenty."

"If you will show me, I will gather the grasses," Malitsa offered. "I want to learn how to make baskets, too."

"We will go today to gather tall mountain grasses and I will show you how to choose them," Mother told her. "Then when the powerful cold wind comes your grandmother will teach you to make baskets."

"Will it be soon?" Malitsa wanted to know.

"Yes. Grandmother will teach you soon," Mother replied. "Already you have learned many womanly tasks. You must keep on with this work. You are doing well. Grandmother has watched. She knows you are ready. When the outdoor season is over your lessons in basket weaving will begin."

"Oh, Mother, I am so happy," exclaimed Malitsa. "I could dance and sing."

"A refined lady holds her happiness within herself," Mother said quietly. "Only her face smiles with joy."

Malitsa's face showed great joy and her brown eyes danced even though her feet must not.

Leaving Swaloos and a relative to tend the fires by the drying meat, Mother and Malitsa climbed up toward the mountain where tall grasses waved in the breezes that played about the meadows.

"Now, these are the ones," Mother said, showing her daughter. "We will gather only the tallest and strongest. Place them carefully in a pile. When we are through we will carry them back to our camp and lay them out to dry."

Malitsa walked about gathering the nicest looking grass.

Near a rock slide where boulders large and small had slipped away from the mountain, she stopped to look around.

"Look, Mother," she cried, pointing, "someone is drying grasses on those rocks." Mother looked quickly. But her keen eyes saw things Malitsa had missed.

"Do you see the hole between the rocks near the drying grasses?" Mother asked.

"Yes, I do," Malitsa replied, after looking carefully, "and there is a little path leading to the hole."

"It is the home of the mountain whistler," Mother told her. "He is a small gray animal about the size of a beaver. He burrows underground to make his home. He has many connecting runs underneath the rocks. During the summer he cuts grasses and the bear grass leaves. He spreads them in the sunshine until most of the moisture has been drawn out by the sun. When the grasses are cured just right he takes them into his home under the rocks and stores them for winter food. Deep snows cover his little home during the long winter time so he can not go out to find food. He must prepare for winter before snow time."

"I wish I could see him," Malitsa said.

"Perhaps you might," Mother said. "Come." They went down the hillside a little way from the whistler's hole and Mother said, "Now watch for him." And she gave a long, steady shrill whistle. They watched the hole in the rocks. Mother whistled again. Still there was no movement at the opening.

"Look," Mother whispered, "way up, farther in the rocks. See him?"

Malitsa looked searchingly at the large gray boulders. "Oh, I see him now," she said softly. "He is so hard to see. He is just the color of the rocks. But how did he get out of his hole? I did not see him come out."

Mother smiled. "He has more than one hole to get in and out of his burrow. He is a smart fellow."

Mother whistled again. This time the little animal sat up on his haunches and answered the whistle. Malitsa laughed. The noise startled the whistler and he disappeared behind a rock. Malitsa said, "Oh," in disappointment. But the whistler appeared again farther up the hillside. The little animal sat upright and whistled long and loud, as if to say, "You do not belong here. Go away."

The Indian mother and daughter did not go away until they had gathered a large load of basket grasses. Then they tied them with a packing strap and fastened the loads on their backs with the strap resting across their foreheads. They went down the hill to their camp.

"We will put the grasses here," Mother told Malitsa, spreading them thinly where the full sun would shine on them next day. "We will leave them here for the sun to come again. Then when he sleeps again, and comes once more, we will turn them to cure the other side. After they have turned yellow and are thoroughly cured, we will pack them away to take home."

"I like to help prepare for winter," Malitsa told her mother.

"That is good," replied Mother. "Now we must see to the evening meal. Would you like to put wood on the cooking fire?"

"Oh, yes," Malitsa answered, running toward the fire used for cooking their meals. She gathered wood and placed it carefully on the hot coals. Soon bright flames danced merrily. Malitsa was proud of her fire. She believed she had learned the secret of placing the wood just right.

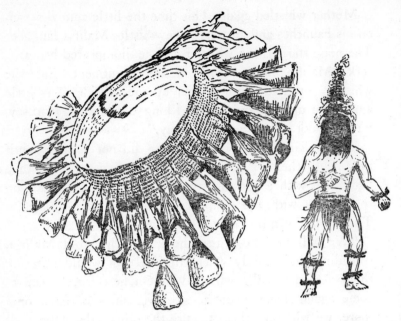

DEER HOOF ANKLET

Chapter XV

THE HUNTING GAME

THE NEXT DAY Malitsa helped her mother again. This time there was fresh deer meat to be cut into strips and placed on the drying racks. The deer tallow was saved as the elk tallow had been, also the bones, antlers, and hide. The small dark hoofs of the deer were saved especially for ornaments. They were strung on rawhide thongs and dried. The Indians wore clusters of these dried hoofs around their wrists and ankles for ceremonial dancing. The hoofs made a clacking sound in time to the rhythmic stepping. Clusters of them were also hung on the power stick, a special stick which gave added power during ceremonies.

The fires must be kept burning to dry the meat, so the

(72)

boys were very busy gathering wood. Malitsa helped her mother and learned.

She poked among the burning chunks of alder wood and a fresh gust of smoke rolled up. The girl was pleased. Her mother smiled, too.

"The smoke came just as I hoped it would," said Malitsa.

"That is fine," Mother replied. "We women know just how to place the wood to make the most smoke. You are learning."

Mother carefully examined the drying strips of elk. She turned them so they would dry evenly. She took each strip in her hands and bent it back and forth, then put it back.

"This is to keep it soft," Mother explained. "It does not dry so hard if it is worked while drying." Malitsa helped. She was careful not to miss one piece as she moved along the rack. Mother watched her to be sure she did it right. And she was pleased with her child's carefulness.

These busy days went on with the men hunting and bringing in the game while the women and children gathered grasses and berries and barks for herbs, and tended the drying meat. The hides were not taken care of here in the temporary camp. They were dried to take home, there to be finished. The deer brains were also dried to take home to be used in tanning the hides.

One evening when Father returned to camp, he called Malitsa to him. "I have something for you," he said.

The girl smiled happily. "What is it, Father?"

Father handed her a fungus, saying, "It is the fungus from the mountain hemlock tree. Mother will help you prepare it for face paint."

"Oh, thank you, Father," cried Malitsa. "Grandmother gave me her powder bag to bring. Now I will have some powder to take home to her."

Malitsa ran to show her mother. "We will bake the fungus by the fire," Mother said. "After it is baked, we will grind it between stones until it is powder. Later the powder will be mixed with elk tallow. Then it will be ready to use to beautify the face."

After many days of work the time of returning home drew near. The Indians were satisfied with their work. They would have plenty of dried meat and berries to store away in their houses at home. They would have grasses for many baskets, new ornaments, hides for clothing and many other things to show for a good hunting trip.

One morning Father beat on his small tom-tom and the men gathered about him to listen. "The sun will come once and then again," he told them, "and we will start down the river. But first we will have the hunting game after the sun goes to sleep."

Every one knew what the hunting game meant and they were happy. Even the children knew. Back home they had heard the men tell of the game. They had seen the pitch knots already saved for the torch.

Swaloos was watching his father speak to his people. When he heard his father announce the game, he began to wish he might be allowed to go. But of course he would be told he was not yet old enough. No use to ask.

During the day Swaloos watched the men make ready for the game. They took a pole much taller than their heads, and at the top tied a pitch knot securely.

After the evening meal the men sat around the fire waiting for darkness to settle down. The women and children sat listening to the men talk of their hunting experiences. Malitsa listened politely though she was not as interested as her brother. He listened to every word. It must be wonderful to be a hunter, he thought. If only he might be allowed to go with them. He knew he could be careful. When he played hunting he always watched the dry leaves and twigs so he would not make a noise.

Father talked with the other men, seeming not to notice

the boy at all. Darkness filled in between the trees and spread out over the camp. It was almost dark enough to light the pitch torch. Swaloos' heart seemed to be beating up in his throat as the men began moving about.

Father put his hand on Swaloos' shoulder. He spoke, "My boy, for your bravery in shooting at the cougar, you may go with the men tonight."

The boy's eyes grew large as he looked at his father. He could hardly believe he had heard right.

"You mean . . . I am old enough . . . to go with the men?" he asked, scarcely breathing.

"We shall see. You may try," Father replied. "But if you can not follow do not be discouraged."

Swaloos had to swallow many times before he could speak. "Thank you, Father, so much!"

"You will need leggings," Father told him. "Mother will fix something for you."

The boy ran to their shelter to find his mother. "Mother, oh Mother, I am going on the hunt!" he cried.

"Yes, my son," Mother replied in a happy voice. "Your father and I are proud of our brave boy. You are young to be allowed to go, but you are to have the chance."

She brought a pair of buckskin leggings belonging to Father and helped Swaloos put them on. "They are much too large," Mother said, "but we can fix them."

"Oh," said the boy, "I do not mind. I will look like a man."

Father came to see if Swaloos were ready. "Bring the straps and I will wrap the legs to fit," Father told Mother. She brought long woven straps and Father wrapped them around and around the child's legs. At last he was ready.

"You must walk behind the torch bearer, my son," Father said, "and do not make any noise."

"I will be very careful. I am so happy to go," he replied. The men were lighting the torch and all were ready to

(75)

start. The torch bearer went first and Swaloos walked behind him. Then the hunters came in single file, each carrying his bow and arrows. Swaloos carried his bow and arrows, too.

The torch bearer led the way between the big trees. Darkness seemed to be squeezing in about the circle of light made by the torch. Swaloos looked into the darkness. He felt lonely, even with the men coming behind him. He looked into the darkness again and stumbled over a root. Oh, he thought, I must not do that again. Father did not scold him. They walked on and on.

The way seemed long to the boy. They must have been walking for a long time. He was beginning to become tired. Again he stumbled. This time he made more noise. "Careful, son," Father warned, quietly.

"Yes, Father," said Swaloos.

Soon the way was rough and the boy stumbled more and more.

Father signaled the men to halt. Swaloos knew what that meant. He was going to be left. He had heard the story of how they would leave a noisy one behind. His father would hide him in the brush at the foot of a big tree. He would have to stay there until the hunters returned for him. Shame flooded over him. And he was really frightened. He did not want to be left alone. Suddenly he saw two green fires shining out in the darkness.

"Look, Father," Swaloos barely whispered. Father saw the fires, too. They knew an animal was watching them. The light from the torch was reflecting in its eyes.

Father warned the other hunters. He spoke to the torch bearer, who stepped a little way from the others. Then all stood very still. The fires moved closer, a little at a time.

"It is a deer." Father whispered to his son. "See the movement of the eyes as it walks? I can see by the movement that it is a deer. It is curious about the light. It will come close."

The animal came closer and closer, while Swaloos and the men stood without making a sound. Now they could make out the form by the light from the torch. The deer stopped. Swaloos could see it sniffing the air. It must have caught the human scent.

The torch bearer watched closely. The deer sniffed again and lifted its head higher, its ears flicking nervously. Suddenly it sprang, turning sharply about to run. But the torch bearer was ready. He waved the torch back and forth in long strokes, making the shadows of the big trees move back and forth. The deer stopped. And the torch stopped moving. The deer started again. And again the bearer moved the torch back and forth. The deer turned to run in another direction. But the big trees seemed to be moving. The animal stopped in confusion. He did not know which way to run. Then Father aimed his bow and arrow and put an end to the game.

Swaloos followed the leader back to camp. He was very, very tired. He did not care that they would have a big feast the next day. He wanted to rest. He wanted to lie down on his bed of cat-tail mats.

Chapter XVI

HOME AGAIN

ON THEIR LAST DAY at the temporary camp the Indians rested and had a feast of the deer. Mother and the children dug a pit and put stones in it, then built a fire and kept it burning to heat the stones.

While the stones were being heated, the children gathered salal leaves for their mother. It was fun picking the shiny green leaves for there were delicious berries clustered among them and no thorns to prick the eager hands.

As soon as the stones were hot enough, Mother scooped the fire out of the pit and spread salal leaves over the glowing stones. Then she put in the fresh meat and covered it with another layer of salal. The salal would add a particular flavor to the roasted venison. Now she sprinkled water over all, and laid on more salal, then cat-tail cooking mats to hold in the heat and steam. Now she pushed the fire coals and ashes back over the pit and piled on wood to make a big fire.

When the meat was done the Indians feasted and gave thanks for their good fortune in hunting. They were happy. They had no fear of the coming cold season for they were prepared.

Next morning the sun found only wet black coals of deserted camp fires. The Indians had left very early and were now far down the water pathway toward their village. They could travel much faster on the homeward journey because the current of the river would carry them along.

At night they camped, and were up early again in the morning, anxious to push their loaded dugouts fast downstream. But they must watch carefully for hidden boulders and telltale riffles warning of shallow water.

Father guided the canoe around a riffle into a deeper flow. Unexpectedly, a silver fin showed above the muddy surface, and then the glistening round back of a salmon raised up, quivered gently, and disappeared again. In another instant the silvery green body lashed clear of the tumbling water, then with a splash dropped from sight.

"The salmon is on his way home," Father said, quietly, and something in his voice filled the children with awe. "Once, as a tiny fingerling he made his way down this stream to the sea. Now he returns to spawn and die. But his kind lives on. The eggs rest until another warm season comes to hatch them, then the young ones set out for open water. By and by the urge comes and they return home."

The children looked for more salmon. They watched the little ripples and swirls of the current, forever changing, seeming to push one another aside each trying to reach the sea first. Now and then they caught a glimpse of a sleek body in the muddy water, or a pointed silver nose cut the surface of the water.

The canoes traveled down-river with the current until the children noticed how wide the river had become.

"We must be getting near home," Swaloos said to his sister.

Yes, ahead they could see choppy waves, and the strong smell of sea water tingled in their nostrils. They thought how good it smelled.

"Look," cried Swaloos, "seagulls, so many of them fluttering above the water out there!" He pointed.

They saw the silvery birds hovering, then dipping into the water, lifting up again, wheeling. Now the Indians could hear their cries.

"The gulls are coming closer," said Swaloos.

"They are following something," Mother said. "It must be smelt. Watch."

"It is smelt," Father told them.

The flock of noisy birds moved closer and closer, still dipping, rising, circling and dipping again.

Father signaled and all the paddles rested, the dugouts rocking gently on the swells.

Closer came the seagulls, their shrill cries filling the air. A patch of fastly rippling water darted ahead of the gulls. The birds, seeing the Indians, suddenly rose into the air, screaming, scolding. Beside the canoe the water seemed alive with madly dashing tiny silver fish.

"The smelt are running," Father told his family. "They travel in great numbers."

The fish moved on, quickly, and the Indians watched their course by the rippling water. The seagulls followed noisily.

Again Father raised his arm, signaling, and the dugouts surged forward. All were anxious to push their canoes on to the home beach.

Malitsa was the first to see the smoke of the home camp fire. "We are home! We are home!" she cried, softly. Her brother joined in the cry and they made a song of it."

"The waiting ones see us," Mother said. "Look, the camp fires are burning brightly."

The children waved their arms. They could see movement around the fires. They wanted to shout but they knew Father and Mother would not like that.

As the canoes pulled up to the shore, all those in the village came down to meet the travelers. They were singing the welcome song. Everyone was glad. The old people were pleased to see so much dried meat being unloaded. They knew they would not be hungry when the cold days were upon them.

The old people had done their share of work too. They had gathered in piles of wood for winter use.

"We brought you lots of basket grass, Grandmother," said Malitsa.

"Ah," Grandmother replied, "you and I will make many baskets, my fair one."

Malitsa smiled. She could hardly wait to begin. "May we start right away?" she asked Grandmother.

"No, there is yet work to be done before winter comes," Grandmother answered her. "When the outside work is done we will start."

"Oh," sighed Malitsa, frowning, "I wish we could start now."

Grandmother saw the frown on her face. "My young one, you must not frown. If you frown while you are young, those lines will grow on your face. Then when you are old your face will look fierce and ugly."

The girl was ashamed.

"Always keep your face happy," Grandmother advised, "and all the wrinkles of age will be happy ones."

Malitsa looked at her grandmother. What Grandmother said must be true. She had many wrinkles and lines on her face but she looked happy and sweet. Then Malitsa said, "I will remember, Grandmother, because I want to look like you."

Grandmother smiled, happy for those words.

"Oh, Grandmother, I have something for you," cried the girl, searching through her own basket. "Here it is." And she handed the little buckskin bag to the old lady, red dust sifting out on her hand.

"Did you find the fungus?" Grandmother asked.

"No, Father brought it to me in camp," Malitsa replied. "But while we were out walking Mother showed me on which kind of trees to look for it. Mother also helped me bake the fungus in the camp fire. And when it was done, I ground it into powder all by myself."

Grandmother opened the bag, took a pinch of the dust between her thumb and finger, and rubbed. She looked at Malitsa. "You have ground it well," she said.

"Mother said it must be very smooth," the girl told her.

"I am proud of your thorough work, my child," smiled Grandmother. "Some time soon I will show you how to use the powder."

Malitsa was very happy. She felt more grownup already.

Next day the women stored their new foods away on the shelves beside the other baskets of dried foods and materials for the winter.

DRYING AND PREPARING HIDES FOR TANNING

Chapter XVII

SMELT COME TO THE BEACHES

EARLY NEXT MORNING Mother set to work on the new skins
they had brought down from the mountains. She was going
to tan them. They were very dry now and must be soaked in
water until soft. She and the children carried water in the
water baskets and put the hides to soak.

When they had become softened, Mother would hang

them over a pole to drain so she could scrape them clean with a sharpened deer rib. She would make a liquid of dry deer brains and warm water, and the skins would be soaked in this for a time. Then they would be washed clean of that liquid and wrung by twisting between two sticks and rubbing dry.

Mother would stretch each skin on a frame, and with a round stick, work and work on it. She would take the skin between her hands and scrub it, then pull and stretch to soften it. The tanning of hides would last over many, many days. Mother would work on them in her spare time.

After Mother had the skins in to soak she walked down to the beach. The tide was coming high.

"Ah, smelt," Mother said as she came closer to the water's edge. She saw spots where the surface of the water was rough with many tiny squirming fish. She hurried back to her house, returning immediately with a short, thin cedar board and a basket. Her two children ran along ahead of her. Mother waded into the shallow water and began flipping the tiny fish up onto the shore.

"Gather them into the basket, quickly," Mother told the children, "before they flop back into the water."

The children hopped about grabbing the fish as soon as Mother flipped them onto the sand. They laughed happily. This was great fun. They did not always catch the quick fish immediately. And sometimes the slippery little things squirmed loose from their brown hands.

A great space around Mother seemed alive with darting silver smelt. Mother must work fast while the water was thick with fish. The children had to hurry to save all of them.

Sometimes, though, the water was still and no fish broke the smooth surface. Then Mother looked about, watching for a spot of ripples to show where she could find more smelt. As soon as she saw another rippling of the water, she hurried to it and flipped as fast as she could work her board.

The children brought the basket, which was now becoming heavy.

Gradually, as the tide began to back away, Mother could find the smelt less and less often. Finally she said to the children, "That is all at this tide. With each incoming tide we will come for smelt."

"Oh, good," the children cried, "this is fun! See how many we have caught, Mother."

"Fine," Mother replied, "we shall have soup and have some left over to dry."

They washed the sand from the smelt in the basket and started back to their house.

They saw some seagulls rise on flapping wings up off the bare muddy beach.

The gulls circled round and round, then one dropped something onto the rocks. He stopped in mid-air and with the aid of his wings, began dropping to the beach. A cracking noise sounded and the gull landed and began eating. The others came down at him, screaming loudly.

"He dropped a clam on the rocks to break its shell," Mother said. "Now he is eating the meat from inside and the others want it. Soon the gulls will fly out and look for more clams."

"Who has moved the fishing gear?" they heard Father say, loudly.

The children knew they had not but they wondered who had done such a thing. Father must be angry. He did not allow anyone to touch his fishing gear. They saw Grandmother going toward him.

"I moved your gear, my strong man who was once my little boy," the old woman said, smiling. "I mended your line and made some new for you while you were away hunting."

Father looked ashamed. He felt like a small boy again,

as if his mother were young and she had caught him in a wrong.

"My dear mother," he said, "you were always wiser than I."

"I wanted to do my share," said Grandmother.

"Your help is greatly needed, my mother," said Father. "We could not get along well without you."

That pleased Grandmother very much, for if the day came when the very old felt they were no longer needed, it made them unhappy.

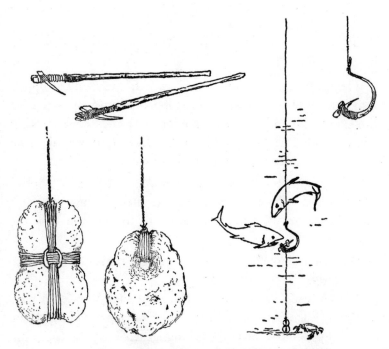

FISHING "GAFFS," HOOKS, AND STONE SINKERS

Father gathered up his nettle fiber line, hooks, sinkers and gaff and took them down to his canoe. Swaloos followed.

"May I help you, Father?" the boy asked.

"No, not yet, my son," Father answered. "You wait and

watch. It takes skill to coil the line perfectly. It must be placed so as to uncoil evenly after I cast the hook and sinker into the sea."

Swaloos watched his father and it seemed simple. But he knew it was not. He had once seen an older boy coiling his father's line. Later the man had to come in because the boy had not coiled it just right and the line had become tangled. The man had been harsh with his son for he had missed the fishing that day.

Remembering that, Swaloos was content to watch. He saw Father slowly and carefully lay one turn of nettle line upon another. When he was coming near the end, Father fastened on the stone sinker. He left a length of line and then on the end he secured the bone hook and placed all carefully in his canoe. He laid the gaff where it would be handy when needed. Swaloos knew not a thing must be touched.

Now Father had everything in readiness to fish for the big silver salmon which swam deep in the cold salt water beyond the points.

Chapter XVIII

SILVER SALMON RUN

MISTY GRAY DAWN hovered over the village the next morning. The sun had not yet peeked its golden head above the far eastern mountains. Father was awake and left his bed so quietly that no others heard him.

In the dim light Father found his cedar dugout. In it was his fishing gear all ready for use. He pushed his canoe from shore and paddled away, silently.

The deep green water lapped at the sides of the black dugout as it skimmed along with the dip and push, dip and

FATHER FISHING

push of Father's paddle. Far out from the Indian village Father laid aside his paddle and let out his line.

From the coil of nettle fiber line in the bottom of the canoe, he carefully lifted his hook. The hook was two pieces of bone, crossed and bound tightly together with cedar thong. One piece of the bone was sharpened to take the bait. At Father's feet was a small water-tight basket, and from it he picked a squirming smelt. He had saved a basket of the live fish from those Mother and the children had caught the day before. The live bait was fastened on the hook. Then Father threw it into the water. The weight of the stone sinker pulled at the line as Father began to paddle away.

When a number of coils had unwound and slipped over the edge, Father stopped the line but kept paddling on. Deep down on the end of the line the tiny body of the smelt flashed silver in the green water. On and on Man-With-Piercing-Eyes paddled, trolling, his gear following.

Golden light and red clouds painted the sky. Father watched morning come over the mountains. Still he paddled on, swung the canoe in a large circle and paddled back, finally the line jerked, then pulled hard. Something had taken the bait. Father braced himself and played the line, back and forth, a mad dash one way, then a slack, and a mad dash another way.

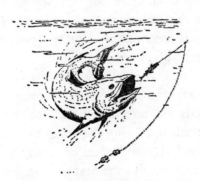

"SOMETHING HAD TAKEN THE BAIT"

Slowly, hand over hand, Father pulled in the line. Then let it out as it pulled hard from him. Now again pulling in, slowly. The sun was well up when Father finally brought the big silvery-green fish alongside. "A silver salmon," breathed the Indian man. "Ah!"

He raised his bone tipped gaff, and with a thrust, took hold of the big fish and hauled it into the dugout. The sleek body lay still, its green and silver scales glistening. Father made for his village, then, paddling steadily. His people would be glad.

When Father was within hearing of the village he began a song. Across the water, ahead of the canoe, traveled the song, and those in the village heard.

"Listen!" cried Swaloos, who had been watching for Father. "The song of the silver salmon!"

The people began to sing and walk toward the beach. The children were excited, they wanted to shout their song. But no, they must sing happily but quietly in a sort of prayer. All were thankful. The Great-One had sent more food to them.

Two men waded into the shallow water, one on each side of the canoe. They took firm hold on the sides and pushed. The bow of the canoe grated on the gravel and held. Father stood and called to an older boy who was near. The boy put his hand to his chest and looked about him as if to make sure he had heard his name spoken. Father spoke again, and the young man stepped forward.

"You may carry the salmon, Good-Luck-Boy," Father said, "for you are strong and soon to become a man."

The honored one carefully lifted the big salmon onto his arms, right side up, taking the upper fin between his teeth. He walked slowly toward a bed of ferns which the women had made ready to receive the first salmon. Father came next behind the boy and the other people followed, all singing.

Mother and some helpers wiped the fish with clean moss

and ferns. They prepared it for roasting while other women prepared more food. The men talked in low voices while they waited for the feast in honor of the first catch of fall fishing.

When the feast was laid out, each person was given a piece of the salmon. But before they started to eat, a special piece was thrown into the fire to offer thanks and to ask for a good fishing season. Then all ate heartily. After the feast all the bones were gathered and cast into the sea as an omen for good.

Now the fishing went on, day after day. The men brought the fish in, and the women took care of them, cleaning and preparing them for drying. The fish were opened with a mussel-shell knife. The layers of eggs were carefully removed to be saved. The eggs were spread on rough cedar mats to dry. The salmon were hung on the drying racks over the fires. The smell of salmon and smoke drifted with the shifting sea breezes.

Dried salmon and dried salmon eggs made up most of the meals for these Indians. The dried eggs had other uses as well. Glue was made from them. The eggs were crushed

DRYING SALMON

(91)

with a pestle and bowl, then water added. This glue could be made into paint, also, by mixing powdered colored earth into it.

During the drying, the women must tend the fish by turning and bending the pieces to keep them soft.

The children kept up their share of the work by gathering wood to keep the smoke rolling up around the racks.

When Mother had told them it was time to bring the wood for the drying fires, they started toward a big pile of bark from the fir tree.

"No, children," Mother said. "Remember we do not burn fir bark to dry fish. We burn wood from the alder tree. Alder makes the fish sweet and tender when it is dry. Come, I will show you which wood to bring."

Swaloos and Malitsa went with their mother to a place where alder trees grew. It was not far from the village. Mother showed them the right wood to gather. Each day they must bring enough wood to keep their mother's fire burning.

The children were surprised that their wood pile was used so fast. They must work harder than ever to bring more alder. Other children of the village carried alder, too. All the families were fishing and drying. The children made a game of their work. As they brought the alder they sang a song to the alder tree. It was fun. They tried to see who could bring the most wood. But no one ever really won because their mothers kept putting the wood on the fires.

As soon as the salmon were thoroughly dry, they were taken down to make room for more. The dry fish were packed in large baskets which had been woven especially for storing them. The baskets had covers of cedar bark mats. These large baskets of dry fish were put away on a high shelf inside the house. There were also containers for the dry salmon eggs.

The Indians prepared much more of this food than they

would need for themselves. Before long their friends from the mountains would come to trade. They would bring mountain goat wool and hides to trade for sea foods. Mother and Grandmother wanted more wool for weaving so they worked hard to store extras.

For days the men fished early and late and the women cared for the fish while the children brought wood for the fires. All the village was busy.

Chapter XIX

GATHERING COLORS

THE INDIAN MOTHER was thinking of all the work she had done for the coming of cold days. She must make sure she had not forgotten anything. Soon the cold winds would begin to blow and then she would not want to leave her warm home.

There were many dried foods stored on the high shelf. Cedar bark for clothing and mats was packed away. Cat-tail leaves had been gathered and cured for winter weaving. Nettle bark was ready to make fish nets and cord. Barks of shrubs and herbs had been dried for medicine. There were plenty of basket materials put away for winter work.

"Ah," said Mother. She remembered something she had not done. "I must go for red and yellow earth to make paint."

The children were playing along the beach when they heard their mother call. They answered and went quickly, not wanting to be called a second time.

"Children," said Mother when they came to her, "we will go in my canoe to gather earth for red paint."

"Where do we go?" asked Swaloos.

"Far along the beach toward the cold wind's home," Mother answered. "Come, we must go immediately. The day is still new and we will have time to gather a great deal."

"May I bring your paddles?" Swaloos asked.

"Yes, my son," Mother replied. "Are you sure you know which are mine?"

"Oh, yes, I know by the shape," the boy smiled proudly. "I know which belong to Father, too, and I know which are his racing paddles."

"I know them, too," said Malitsa.

Swaloos ran to bring his mother's paddles. Malitsa and Mother took the baskets and walked down to the small canoe. They all pushed to get it off the sand and into the water.

"I think we will let Malitsa paddle for us this time," Mother said. "Would you like to?"

"Oh, yes!" Malitsa exclaimed.

"Then Swaloos, you take your place in the bow," Mother said, getting into the canoe. "I will sit midway." Mother settled herself, then thrust her paddle tip into the sand to steady the canoe while Malitsa climbed in. She was careful not to cause the canoe to dip water. But there was always a canoe bailer in the canoe to bail the water out whenever needed.

The cedar dugout rode lightly. Malitsa dipped the paddle and pushed as she had seen her mother do. But the canoe did not slide along as she thought it should, and sometimes the paddle splashed water as it came down.

"Turn it just so," Mother explained, taking the paddle to show the girl exactly how it should be done. Soon she could make the dugout travel faster. She was very pleased.

Malitsa dipped and pushed, and the canoe slipped along. After a while Mother said, "I will do the paddling now. I think you have done enough for this time."

"My arms are tired," Malitsa admitted. She stood up to change seats.

"Do not stand up," Mother said quickly. "See, hold on to the sides as I do and come slowly and carefully. The canoe will not tip if we are careful. It is very easy to be thrown into the water."

Malitsa did as she was told. They exchanged places and Mother made the canoe skim along. A slough could be seen emptying into the salt water.

"Do we go up the slough?" asked Swaloos.

"No," Mother replied, "not this one. Another day we

(95)

will come to this slough for yellow earth. Today we will gather only red. We must go farther along."

"I thought we would gather both red and yellow," said the boy.

"The two colors are not found in the same place," Mother explained. "One slough has yellow and another has red earth along its banks. And some sloughs do not have either color. It is the work of the women to know where to gather earths for paint."

"I am glad to come so I will know about gathering paints," said Malitsa.

"Yes," Mother told her, "you must pay close attention. You must learn many things today. First you must learn where to go. Then you must learn how to know the best clay for paint. We do not take all the clay as we find it. We search for the brightest colors."

They had come to another slough. Mother turned the canoe into it. They had not gone far until they could see red mud along the banks.

"See, children, there is red earth," said Mother pointing to the colored mud.

"Shall we stop here?" the children asked.

"No, this mud is not good clean color. Farther along it is much better," Mother told them.

The water became shallow, with more red mud showing. Its color was brighter. Mother pushed the canoe onto the bank and they all climbed out.

The children set to work scooping up handfuls of the wet clay.

"Wait," Mother told them, "do not take all as you come to it. Look carefully for the finest and cleanest. Do not let twigs and old leaves get mixed in it."

They were more careful but Mother had to speak to Swaloos about his clay. There were some twigs in it. Malitsa was very particular and saw that she had the best she could find. This pleased Mother for she knew Malitsa would always do her woman's work well.

Finally, Mother saw by the baskets that they had gathered plenty and the sun told them it was time to start homeward.

"We will spread the clay on boards," Mother told them on the way home, "and place them in a slanting position to drain. Then we will pat it into cakes. The cakes must be baked in the fire until they are very hard. The red color becomes brighter, too. After they are baked hard enough they are stored away until needed. To prepare the red clay for use, we put some on a flat stone and with another stone, grind it into powder."

"How did you know all these things, Mother?" asked Malitsa.

"My mother and my grandmother taught me," Mother replied. "Another day we will gather yellow clay. It does not need to be baked by the fire. The sun will dry it. Then it can be powdered and mixed for use."

"I know about black," said Swaloos. "Father told me about it. Black paint is made from charcoal of vine maple or alder wood. It is also ground into powder."

"That is right. There is also white," said Mother. "It is made like the yellow. These are not paints for the face. These are for painting wood. To made paint, dried salmon eggs are mashed and cold water added to form a glue. The powdered clay is added to the glue. It will cling to the wood and when dry it becomes hard."

"I would not like that on my face," said Malitsa.

"We never put that kind of paint on our faces," Mother explained, laughing. "The paint for our faces comes from the mountains. It is much better up there. Sometimes our friends bring it down to trade. That powder is mixed with deer or elk tallow, because tallow keeps the skin soft."

"I see the home fires!" exclaimed Swaloos.

"Yes, we are almost home again," said Mother.

Chapter XX

FRIENDS COME TO TRADE

THE INDIAN WOMEN were putting wood on their fires. It was time to prepare the evening meal. The children were playing. The men were working about the village.

Father heard strange noises in the woods. He listened. It seemed as if he could hear many feet walking. It might be the enemy, he thought. Quickly he gave a warning, a bird call.

The older children knew the meaning of that call. They hurried the smaller ones to their mothers. The mothers hurriedly gathered them into their homes. The men, young and old, came hastily. They went for bows and arrows and other weapons. If the enemy were coming they must be prepared.

The sound came nearer and nearer. Surely the enemy would come silently. These must be friends. The Indians stood guard until they were sure. They would not be misled.

Swaloos' father stood outside his door watching. His keen eyes peered toward the sounds. He saw an Indian man appear. Then another and another and many more. Women were coming, too. And some children. Children would not be along if these people were enemies. Then Father recognized his friends from the mountains. He raised his hand in welcome and went to meet them.

One man stepped out ahead of the visitors to greet Father. He, too, made the sign of friendship. These Indians had visited before.

The other men of the village came out of their hiding places. They knew when their leader gave the friendly greeting that all was well. The women and children came out of the houses.

By sign the visitors told Swaloos' father they had come to trade. Father invited them to the camp fires. Father called loudly to the women, "Prepare food for our friends!" He called loudly so all the visitors would hear and feel welcome. And to the guests Father said, "What we have is not much but you are welcome to it."

The guests knew they must eat the food set for them, for if they did not, the hosts might be offended. The hosts always tried to please their guests and give them foods they liked.

Immediately the women began to prepare their best food. Hosts must always be proud of what they serve their guests, no matter how humble the food.

Malitsa and the other girls spread the eating mats. They brought the best bowls and spoons. They put out soft shredded cedar bark for napkins. When all was ready the mothers set the food on the mats. The men sat together and were given the best. The women ate together, and they served the children.

Then all offered thanks. Each Indian lifted his right hand, palm facing outward to front. The Indian did not bow his head in thanks. His food was especially blessed because it meant life.

When they had finished eating, a drummer began to beat his drum softly, and the visitors sang a "thank you" song to their hosts, keeping time by tapping their spoons against their bowls.

The women and girls cleared away the food and dishes. The men gathered around the fires to visit and exchange hunting stories. They talked by sign and words, for each tribe had a different language, with only a few words alike.

Beds must be prepared for the visitors. The women brought out extra cat-tail mats and spread them on the bed shelves. Some of the visitors slept with friends in the smaller houses, but many of them slept in the large house of the

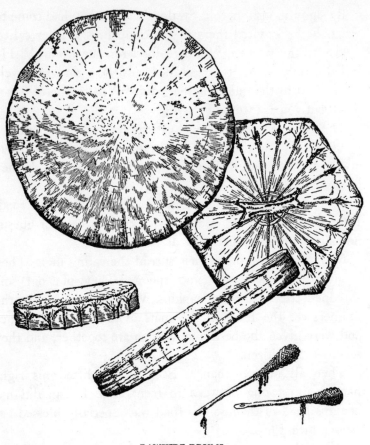

RAWHIDE DRUMS

Chief. They had brought robes with them and they spread these over the cat-tail mats. When all was ready the small children were willing to cuddle down into their beds. The women and older girls went back to the fires. Malitsa and Swaloos were very glad when they were allowed to sit with the older people for a while.

The Chief and his people danced and sang for their guests. Then the visitors sang and danced, too. The songs and dances told stories. The moon had climbed far across the sky when the Indians all went to their beds.

Swaloos and Malitsa were not so anxious to get up early the following morning. The older people were sleeping later, too. Only the very small children were up with the sun.

After the morning meal was over, Swaloos' grandfather sent a man from house to house, beating a drum. He told all about the trading which would take place at the Chief's house. Those who lived in the village were to bring out their extras to trade with the people from the mountains.

Soon all were gathered before the Chief's door. Grandfather held up his hand and made a long talk to his friends. He welcomed the visitors for trading. He told of the goodness of the Great-Man who created all the people. There was plenty of food. There was health and happiness among his tribe. Then he invited the visitors to bring forth what they had to trade.

One by one the visitors began to lay out the articles they had brought to trade, one or two at a time. The trading was done in a very slow manner. It was like a game with them, each wondering what the other still had hidden. The home Indians also brought out things they had ready for trading. When one saw something he wanted, then he made an offer, being careful that it was enough to keep the respect of the other trader.

There was a bag of wool Malitsa's mother wanted to weave into a blanket and she brought strings of dried clams to trade. Grandmother saw different grasses for basket work and she offered some of her special cedar root thongs she had ready for use. There were many skins of fur from the mountain animals to be made into shoulder capes and robes for the beds.

The trading went on all day. The visitors had brought colored arrowheads from far away tribes, powders for face paints, fiber cord to be used in making fish nets even stronger than those of nettle fiber, more wool was brought out and ornaments for decorating clothing. In exchange, the visitors wanted especially the dried seafoods, the big shining white clam shells for dishes, mussel shell knives, and the small pink shells for ornaments. The home Indians offered some carved dishes.

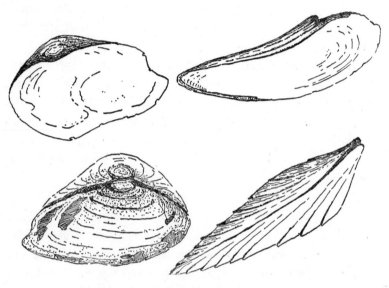

MUSSEL SHELLS USED FOR KNIVES AND SCRAPERS,
CLAM SHELLS FOR CUPS AND DISHES

Then Father's friend showed him some whitened elk skins. All along Father had known there must be something special that would be brought out later. Father felt how soft and pliable the skins were and knew great skill had gone into the treatment of these elk hides. This was what Father had been waiting to see. While he looked over the skins he was pondering in his mind how many strings of his precious hyakwa shells he should offer.

He talked of other things with his friend, and they looked away to the sea and to the woods, but each knowing that this was the big trade of the whole day. Father thought back to what he had had to give to his northern sea-going neighbors to obtain the hyakwa shells in the first place. For hyakwa, they had told him, was not easy to find, especially the long fine shells. They must go far out to where the rocky, long points of land extend into the sea, where the mighty ocean rolls and roars. But they must be there when the ocean is low and peacefully quiet. Then they must probe down under the water where the rocks and sand meet. The woman worked the canoe while the man used a long handled rake to drag the sands beneath the water. The slender shells were scarce and it took much raking to get enough to make a string. The size varied also, the larger the shell the higher the value. Sometimes the rake brought out shells as long as the small finger, but usually they measured by the first and second joints of the finger, and of twig thickness. Father had traded and saved until he had several strings hidden away. He need not rob himself, he decided, to give his friend a fair exchange.

Father brought out two strings of good sized hyakwa. His friend lifted the strings, testing their weight. Slowly he ran the loop across his hand, looking at each shell. Then he nodded, and said, "Good." He draped the strings of money shell around his neck while he handed the beautiful white hides to Father.

When the trading was over the Indians were friendly and a special feast was prepared for the guests. Fish from the salt water had been caught for the feast especially because the mountain Indians did not have salt water fish where they lived.

Then there were games for all. The women played among themselves, and the men had their games. The older boys and girls played a laughing game. The boys took one side and the girls took a side. Each side had a pile of sand, the two piles some distance apart. In the top of each sand pile stood a stick. One side came forward and dared to take the stick. The other side tried to make them laugh. If they laughed they had to go back to their base and the others came to dare.

The men and women, sitting in rows or in a circle, played their games with pieces of bone or beaver teeth. It was a guessing contest.

The small boys had races and bow and arrow shooting. The girls had dolls of clam shells and cedar bark.

As darkness came the fires were piled high with wood and made to burn brightly.

All were up very early the next morning, for the visitors were making ready to start on their journey back to the mountains. When breakfast was over the visitors sang a special thank-you song. They had enjoyed their visit and were satisfied with the trading.

As the mountain people, with their packs, started on the trail toward home and the rising sun, the salt water people sang a farewell song. They wished their friends a pleasant journey and invited them to return some day.

Chapter XXI

RAIN

ONE MORNING the old Chief stood before his door taking deep breaths of the fresh salt air.

"Ah," he said sniffing, "I smell rain."

Father and Mother and Grandmother came out to sniff the air. They all nodded. The good smell told them that rain was not far away.

"But, Grandfather," said Swaloos, "the sun is shining."

"No matter, my little chief," replied Grandfather, "the time of rain will soon be here. Breathe the air and remember the odor. Listen to the bird calls."

Swaloos did as his grandfather said. The air smelled just the same to him as always. He must remember to smell the air often, he told himself. Many times he had watched his grandfather taking deep breaths but he did not realize until now that his grandfather was smelling for the weather.

The boy listened to the bird calls. They were different. The birds sounded lonely and their voices seemed nearer and louder. It made him feel lonely, too.

"See," said Grandfather to Swaloos, "the little winds are skipping across the water, first one way and then another. They know rain is on the way. Already mists gather about the mountain peaks. Look, to the south."

Yes, Swaloos could see mists capping the mountains. The sun was not so bright now.

Grandfather brought out his drum and tapped a few beats. It was the rain warning. All in the village knew the meaning of those beats. Soon there was much activity. The women took care of the foods drying outside. These must be ready to move in quickly. The children carried dry wood and bark into the houses. The men climbed upon their roofs to make sure the boards were placed right to shed the rain. The boards should overlap. Then the rain would run down and drip off the edge of the roof. Heavy stones were placed on the boards to make them fast.

When it rained their fires would be built inside the houses. A round place of black coals and gray ash showed on the packed earth floor where the fire would be built. Directly above that place, there was a hole left in the roof so the smoke would drift up through the opening.

The Indians were happy getting ready for rain. They liked the rain. It made them feel good.

The time of rain meant the Indians would begin their indoor work. There might be wet days only for a short time now. Probably the sun would come out again and dry the dampness away. But not for long. The rain would come again and the sun would be hidden behind clouds. The sun and rain would play hide and seek for many sleeps until the cold winds came down from the North. Then snow might come, too.

The Indians knew all these things and made ready for their coming. The animals felt the coming of the cold and were prepared. Many of the birds felt the urge to fly toward warmth in the South. It was the Great-Man who told them all this.

Swaloos had piled dry wood beside his mother's fire place. Then he walked away from the camp. He wanted to learn the smell of the rain coming. He wanted to watch the little animals and listen to the bird calls. All these things he must learn, he told himself, to become a great chief.

The boy was thinking many things to himself as he walked through the woods. He heard a slight scuffle near him and stopped to look. There on an uprooted tree sat a little chipmunk. He was sitting up on his haunches with his tail curled up his back. He was holding something between his front paws. Swaloos looked closely. It was the cone from a fir tree.

The chipmunk was very busy chipping off the outer husks. Then he seemed to have finished for he began eating the inside of the cone. His little jaws worked very fast.

Silently, mirth spread over the boy's face, and he said to the chipmunk in a whisper, "If my grandmother could see you she would tell you not to chew so fast. She would say you are greedy. I wonder if you are eating fast because you know it is going to rain."

As if to answer, the little fellow flipped his tail, chattered shrilly and scampered along the tree trunk. He stopped where a patch of sunlight lay and Swaloos could see hazelnuts drying there.

"He's drying them for winter," Swaloos said to himself. "Just like we dry our foods."

The chipmunk gathered some nuts by their husks and scurried away around a tree and out of sight. Swaloos wondered where he had gone. In a moment the chipmunk was back again. He took another load and darted away.

Swaloos wanted to find where the chipmunk was taking the nuts. The boy must be very quiet to learn the hiding place of the chipmunk. He watched the moss and chose where to set his feet. He was careful not to step on a twig. Twigs are tattletales. They snap and warn the animal people. Swaloos went only a short way and peeked from behind a big tree. He was just in time to see the chipmunk climb out of a hole high up on a dead snag. The little animal ran down the trunk of the old tree and away to the hazelnuts.

The boy kept so still he hardly breathed. Soon the chipmunk was back again. Up the tree he went, with a cluster of nuts between his long front teeth. He disappeared into the hole.

Swaloos laughed softly. He had found the home of the little fellow. He knew the chipmunk had already carried up dry leaves and grass to make a winter bed. He knew there was plenty of food for winter stored in the home, too. Soon the little fellow would climb into his bed and stay there until spring beckoned him out again.

The boy walked on. He came to the stream which gave fresh water to the Indians. The water ran around the rocks. It did not rush and tumble. It was thirsty for the fall rains to come. A breeze rustled above in the trees. Now and then a yellow leaf from an alder tree floated zigzag down to the water. It made a little yellow boat which drifted along on the lazy stream.

Swaloos sat down on the bank to watch the water. He wanted to listen to the woods sounds. He thought of many things. He smelled the air for rain. There was a different odor here. He smelled again. An alder leaf lay beside him. He picked it up and held it to his nose.

"The scent of alder," he told himself. He sniffed again. It made his nose want to pucker inside.

Another leaf, large and smooth and clear yellow caught his attention. He lifted it to his nose.

"Ah, the sweet of the cottonwood," said Swaloos. "It smells of summer." But a stronger breeze sent a shower of leaves down upon Swaloos as if to remind him that it was no longer summer.

"I must go back to the village," the boy said to himself. He walked slowly, thinking of the growing things. The big trees and the little plants growing about him. He thought of the Great-Man who made all things. He wished the Great-Man would speak to him. He wanted to know what his work would be when he became a man. Would he be a medicine man and heal his people? Would he be a carver and make canoes and useful things? Would he be a great hunter? Many questions marched through his mind. "I am not old enough to hear the answer," Swaloos told himself.

As he walked along he saw some little ferns growing on a big maple tree. He pulled one from the moss which helped the fern cling to the tree. He wiped the fern root clean and chewed it as he walked. The bitter sweet flavor was good. He pulled off another piece to take to his sister. She was fond of it, too.

He knew his mother and the other women had already gathered many of these fern roots. They had been dried in the sun, and were now put away on the shelf with the other dried food and barks. This fern root was used when the inside of one did not feel right. It was for medicine.

A gust of wind tore brilliant red leaves from a vine maple near the edge of the woods and tossed them about Swaloos' feet as he walked toward the village. The clouds had hidden the sun. A big drop of water fell on the boy's nose. More followed, making a splop, splop sound as they splattered on the hard ground. Rain had come.

Chapter XXII

THE CHILDREN HAVE LESSONS

GRANDFATHER SAT with his back against the cedar board wall, working.

"What are you making, Grandfather?" asked Swaloos, stopping before the old man. "Oh, I see, it is a bow," the boy answered his own question.

"Yes, I am making a bow," Grandfather replied.

"I would like to make a real bow," Swaloos said, longingly.

"Later you may, but first you must learn to make arrows," Grandfather told him. "There is a piece of wood. Do you want to try an arrow?"

"Oh, yes!" exclaimed Swaloos. "Is this the piece you mean?" He picked up a strip of cedar a little longer than his arm and about as thick as his grandfather's finger.

"Yes, that is it," Grandfather said. "And here is a mussel shell knife to use for scraping."

Swaloos was excited as he sat down beside his grandfather. "Now what shall I do?"

"Now hold the wood just so, and scrape with the knife," said the old man, showing the boy how it should be held. "Notice the grain of the wood? See how straight it is? Now, work carefully, with the grain. Scrape, then turn, scrape, and turn the shaft. Keep on doing that and soon it will become round."

The boy set to work. "You are not scraping with a mussel shell knife," observed Swaloos.

"No, I am through with that work on my bow," his grandfather replied. "I scraped and scraped long before I had the right size and shape. This is yew wood and much harder than cedar. When I had scraped until I was satisfied, I steamed the piece of wood and curved it. After it dried I worked and worked on it with a sand stone to smooth it. Now my bow is being polished. When you have scraped your arrow down with the knife, you will then use a piece of sandstone to smooth and round the shaft."

"How did you make the mussel shell so sharp?" Swaloos wanted to know.

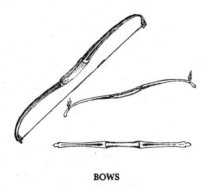

BOWS

"That was done with sandstone, too," Grandfather answered. "Sandstone is harder than shell. It has a rough, gritty surface. I rubbed and rubbed on the shell with the stone until the edge became thin and sharp."

Mussel shell knives had many uses. The women used them in preparing food, to peel the bark of the nettle stalks, to split cedar bark into fine layers, and for scraping. The men used the knives for scraping, also, and especially in hunting.

"I am now using rushes to polish my bow," Grandfather said, showing Swaloos the rough dry grass-like material in his hand. "The rushes were gathered from damp ground where they grow. After drying, they are hard and rough. You will use some to polish your arrow, too." And he continued to rub up and down his new bow. Already the wood looked smooth and shiny. It must have a great deal more rubbing before it would be finished.

While they worked, Grandfather told Swaloos more about how their arrow points and implements were made.

"Sandstone is used in making arrow heads from small bones of deer. A piece of bone is rubbed and rubbed with sandstone. The rough, gritty surface grinds the bone into the size and shape wanted."

"Does it take long?" Swaloos wanted to know.

"It takes great patience," Grandfather replied. "All work takes patience. Always remember that."

"But what about the beautiful colored stone arrowheads you keep in your work basket, the ones you get from our neighbors to the South?" Swaloos asked. "Are those made by grinding?"

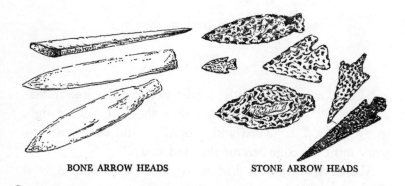

BONE ARROW HEADS   STONE ARROW HEADS

"No, those are chipped," Grandfather replied. "We do not find those stones near our village. We must depend on trading with our friends away toward the rising sun, up the great river. They make arrowheads from black obsidian, flint, and the many-colored stones they find near their home. Once when I was young I went on a journey taking many days, to visit the rising sun people. I saw knives, spearheads and arrowheads being made."

"Tell me about it, Grandfather."

"The chunk of obsidian or stone is shaped by placing it on a big working stone, then by striking it with a maul and turning and striking at different angles the flakes chip off. The man who is skilled knows just how much to turn the piece he is working on. He knows how hard a blow and at what angle he must strike to cause the flakes to shape the article he is making. Sometimes he uses stone mauls of different sizes, then for finishing he taps lightly with the point of an elk antler."

Swaloos sighed. "I wish I could do that some day."

"Sometime you might travel to the home of our friends and see, possibly learn to make such articles," Grandfather told Swaloos. "Our neighbors to the North and up the other great river, make implements from a hard dark green stone. Still other tools, bowls and sinkers for fish lines are made from hard rough gray stones we find close to our home. On our beaches we find them of many different strengths. Some are very hard, some not so hard, and some are soft."

Swaloos laughed. "Who ever heard of a soft stone, Grandfather?"

Grandfather laughed too. "By soft I mean one that will chip or wear away faster than another. Very hard stone is used to work on that not so hard. By grinding and grinding with the hard one, the softer stone will wear into the shape we want."

Swaloos listened while his grandfather told how the different kinds were made into implements they needed. And how elk and deer antlers were used to peck the stones to make holes in sinkers, or to make grooves for wrapping with rawhide or strong bark thongs. The pecking might be done with a very hard sharp stone instead.

"I like working with you, Grandfather."

"We will work together many, many days, little chief," the old one assured him, and went on polishing his new bow. "When I am through polishing, I will string the bow with this nettle bark cord," he said, pointing to a twisted line on the ground beside him. "Your grandmother made it."

And while Grandfather and Swaloos were working with their bow and arrow, Malitsa had found her grandmother at work, also.

"What are you doing, Grandmother?" she asked.

"I am twining nettle bark," the old lady replied. "Do you want to try some?"

"Oh, may I?" Malitsa cried, pleased.

"There are some short pieces for you," Grandmother said. Malitsa took the pieces of nettle bark eagerly. Then she sat down beside the old woman and looked to see how she was holding her work. "See," said Grandmother, "lay the strands across your thigh, take one set of ends in your hand and hold them. Now, with the other hand rub and roll the strands back and forth on your thigh. Watch. Now try."

Malitsa tried. Then she giggled. "I am so awkward."

"Keep trying and it will come to you," Grandmother told her. "I was awkward when my grandmother first showed me, so long ago."

"Is this made from the nettles my mother gathered?"

"Yes. I am too old to go away from the village now. When I was younger we went together to find the best nettles. We chose the tall strong ones because they peeled better. They must be gathered at the right time and cured in the sun. Then we use a mussel shell knife to split and peel off the outer bark in strips. See, when these strands are twisted together they make very strong cord. The cord is used in many ways. For bow strings, fish nets and duck nets, also for weaving."

"I am not doing so well," said Malitsa, looking at her cord. "It does not stay twisted. It unwinds."

"Be patient, my child," Grandmother told her. "All of us had to learn. After more practice it will work better."

Chapter XXIII

BASKET LESSONS

Swaloos and Malitsa stood in the doorway of their home. It had been raining steadily for two sleeps. The sun had hidden itself. Bushes and trees near the camp were dripping with raindrops.

The children watched while a strong breeze scampered about ruffling the water in front of their home. The breeze left the water and blew up past the house. It took hold of the limbs of a big cedar tree and swept them upward. A shower of raindrops shook from the limbs before the breeze hurried on.

The children frowned. "I wish the sun would come again," said Swaloos.

"I do too," said Malitsa. "I'm not sure I like the rain."

"Neither am I," Swaloos replied. "I want to play and I do not like to get wet."

Grandmother heard the children talking. "Oh, shame on you," said the old woman, shaking her head sadly. "The rain brings you food and clothing and health. We would all die without it. You should give thanks for the rain."

"How does the rain bring food and clothing and health?" asked Swaloos.

"The Great-Man sends the rain to make things grow," Grandmother answered. "The trees and plants must have water. Animals must have water, and we must have water, also. The streams would dry up without rain. The big cedars and other trees would die without water. Our clothes come from the big cedars. Cat-tails for our mats come from the wet marshes."

"Does everything need water?" inquired Malitsa.

"Yes, my dears, everything," Grandmother replied. "Rain gives life. You should never say you do not like the rain. The Great-Man would turn His face away to hear you talking so. He would be grieved and sad. When the Great-Man turns His face away and gives a sidewise cross look, you will have very bad luck."

"We are very, very sorry," the children cried together. "We do not want the Great-Man to turn away."

"Always remember to be thankful for all good things," Grandmother said.

Each child went and sat alone to think about what their grandmother had just said to them. They remembered how Father and the other men had sprayed water to the growing things before drinking, to show their thankfulness. They remembered many things they had been taught. The old people were wise. The children must mind what they said. And now, after thinking about it, the boy and girl were thankful for the rain.

Malitsa left the corner where she had gone. She saw Grandmother sitting close to the door, making something.

"What are you making, Grandmother?" Malitsa asked.

"A basket," Grandmother replied. "This is a cedar bark basket. It will be used for storing dried fish. Your father has had such good luck in fishing this year we need more baskets."

"May I watch?" the girl wanted to know.

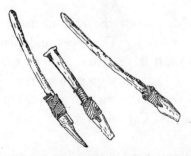

HORN, BONE AND STONE BARK PEELERS

"Of course," Grandmother told her.

While Malitsa watched, Grandmother told her how the cedar bark had been slipped away from the tree with a bark peeler of hardwood. Some bark peelers were made of bone or horn. The outside layer had been stripped off and left in the woods, and the rest brought back to be dried before being stored away.

This bark the old lady was using had been stored and had to be soaked in water to soften before Grandmother could use it. When it had soaked enough, Grandmother split strips the width and thickness she wanted. Then she cut the right lengths for the size of basket she intended to make.

She had placed some strips and had woven the strong bot-

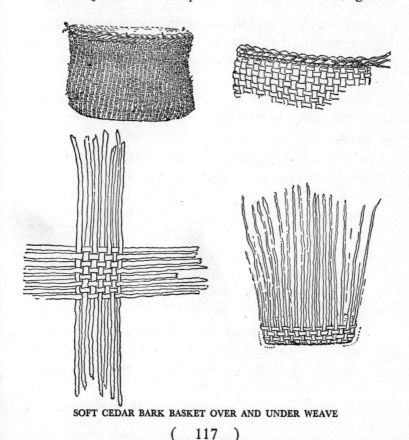

SOFT CEDAR BARK BASKET OVER AND UNDER WEAVE

tom first, leaving ends on each side long enough to turn up for a frame-work to weave the sides of the basket. Then she took a strip and wove it in and out through the upright slats, using another strip after she had finished with one. One strip after another was used until the sides were woven. She wove around and around the basket. The top edge would be finished with a braided design, working in the ends of the slats for strength. The folded over slats would keep the side weaving from slipping off.

The gnarled brown fingers worked steadily. Each strip had its place. She was very careful with her weaving. It must be just right, for Grandmother was noted for her basket work.

When she had finished the basket, Grandmother would lay out material for a mat to cover it. The mat would be woven much like the bottom of the basket but the cedar bark was split thinner. The short ends would be folded and woven in to keep the edges from coming loose. When the mat had been finished it would be left to dry, become stiff and hold its shape.

Sometimes Grandmother wove cedar bark into table mats or mats for drying foods. The strips could be woven in and out in a different manner to change the design.

"Oh, it is such a lot to know," sighed Malitsa.

Grandmother smiled. "No, my child," she said, "it is not much if you learn well. You must learn a step at a time. Take some of these small strips I have left and I will show you how to start a cedar bark basket. But we will not finish yours into a basket. It will be a mat."

Malitsa gathered some strips from the ground at Grandmother's feet. She chose those of the same width and thickness. Grandmother watched, not telling her which to choose.

"Ah," said Grandmother when Malitsa had a number of strips in her hand, "you have the eye of the basket-maker. I have watched you choose the strips. I am very pleased. You will learn quickly, I know."

Malitsa smiled happily. She knew Grandmother always meant what she said. She did not give idle praise.

The old lady showed her granddaughter how to place the strips and how to work them in and out to make a solid bottom.

GRANDMOTHER AND MALITSA AT BASKET WORK

"Now you try," Grandmother said. Malitsa worked carefully. She was very slow. She wanted her first work to be good so Grandmother would be proud of her. She knew it was better to take a longer time and have a perfect basket than to hurry and have a poor one.

Mother had built up the fire and the good smell of cooking food filled the house. It made Malitsa hungry. But she did not want to stop until her mat was finished. She worked faster.

"I will show you how to finish the edge when day comes again," Grandmother said. "My old eyes do not see so well by the firelight."

Malitsa did not want to wait for another day to learn the edging. She was impatient. But she did not let Grandmother know. She remembered that she must always treat the aged with kindness. They must feel they are wanted and needed.

The old lady smiled. She was proud of her granddaughter. Grandmother remembered when she had been an impatient little girl.

Malitsa went over near the fire where her mother was cooking. With pronged sticks, Mother was lifting heated stones from the fire and putting them into a basket of soup. The hot stones made the food boil. As the stones cooled they were taken out and more hot ones put in. Mother kept doing this until the food was cooked.

But the girl was not paying much attention to the cooking food. She was interested in baskets now. She noticed the cooking basket was very different from the one Grandmother had just finished.

"What kind of basket is that?" she asked Mother, pointing to the one being used.

"It is a cedar root basket," Mother replied. "It is made in a very different way from the cedar bark basket. Very few women make these. Your grandmother makes many for the other women of the village. Also for trade. The basket made of cedar roots is water-tight. It is woven so tightly the water can not leak out."

"I want to learn to make those," declared Malitsa.

"Your grandmother will show you after you have learned to make many other kinds," Mother told her. "Narrow strips of strong cedar are peeled from the root. With the use of a bone awl, a hole is made and the cedar root strip is threaded through, looped and knotted. This is done over and over and around and around to make a basket. Grandmother knows the secret of a strong, water-tight basket."

"I hope she will tell it to me," wished Malitsa.

"I am sure she will," Mother told her.

Chapter XXIV

THE PORPOISE CATCH

S<small>WALOOS WAS SLEEPING SOUNDLY</small> in his bed. Father had to shake hard to rouse him.

"Come, come, my son," Father said, shaking him again.

The boy opened his eyes. Surely day had not come yet.

Father said again, "Come, my son."

Swaloos listened to his father. He heard another voice, too. The other voice was like a whisper in his ear. It was saying, "Do not go. I am your friend. I will keep you warm."

"Ah," thought Swaloos, "it is the bed speaking. I am stronger than the bed. I will not let him hold me back. I will get up as my father says." And he jumped right out of bed to show his strength.

"Hurry, my boy, the porpoise are near," Father said.

Mother brought warm clothes for her boy. This would be his first trip for porpoise. He knew what he was to do. His grandfather had told him many times of when he was a boy and had gone with his father. Swaloos was excited.

Mother brought a cape of woven cat-tail rush for the boy's shoulders. Father wore one too. Father had a cat-tail mat under his arm. Mother gave another to Swaloos.

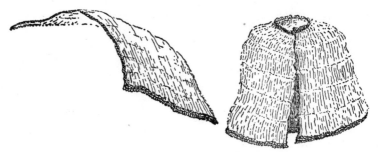

CAT-TAIL CAPE AND KNEE MAT

"It is to spread over your knees," she told him. "The mat and cape will shed the rain and keep you dry. Now you are ready."

Swaloos walked proudly. He had forgotten about being sleepy. He noticed now how dark it was. Day had not come over the mountains.

Other men were going to their canoes. Swaloos was the only small boy. The other boys who were going were older.

They climbed into their cedar dugouts. Swaloos curled up in the bow while his father paddled. The boy had been brought along as ballast. He was to give weight to the bow of his father's canoe. Also to bail water out of the canoe if necessary. And to learn.

Grandfather had told Swaloos that sometimes he slept while his father fished. But Swaloos was too excited to sleep. This first trip he did not want to miss anything.

The boy noticed how his father paddled. He dipped his paddle without making a sound in the quiet water. The canoe skimmed along, silently. Swaloos noticed the soft gray light. Day must be coming closer for grayness had come ahead of the golden sun. Toward the home of the rising sun the boy could see tints of yellow brightening the sky above the mountains.

He could see Father better now. He watched Father hold his paddle clear of the water and stretch his body to look out across the sea. His eyes strained to catch a glimpse of porpoise. Not seeing any sign, Father would continue paddling. Sometimes he stood to take a better look. Always he listened for sounds to tell him porpoise were near.

The boy looked at his father's spear. He wished he could thrust a spear. He knew it required skill. He had seen the older boys practicing. He would have to wait a long time before he learned how. There were floats attached to the spear by a long cord. The floats looked like ducks. They were carved from cedar and were hollow inside.

PORPOISE HUNTING GEAR
HARPOON AND LINE WITH FLOATS

Swaloos had no more time to dream of things he would like to do.

"There!" exclaimed Father in a low voice, "there are porpoise! Many of them!" And he paddled very fast in the direction of a thrashing in the water. Other canoes headed the same way. Swaloos heard a hissing, blowing noise and it made his scalp feel itchy and his breath come faster.

"See all the fish going past the canoe?" Father asked his son. And when the boy looked down into the water around the canoe, he saw many fish. They seemed to be hurrying toward the shore.

"Where are they going?" Swaloos wanted to know. "And why are there so many?"

"They are swimming away from the porpoise. The smaller fish go in close to shore when porpoise are feeding in these waters. The porpoise is large and eats the smaller fish. They are heading for the safety of shallow water."

Then in the early morning light, Swaloos saw a huge black form show above the surface of the water, and disappear. Another and another showed, up again and down, and the boy knew these were porpoises. It made him think

(124)

of the game they played of Blackfish and Seals. Again the big bodies came up. Each time they rose to the surface, they were nearer. They must be curious about the dugouts. Father put aside his paddle and took the spear. The other men began to close in with their dugouts.

Father had his spear ready. A porpoise came near the canoe. With much commotion of the water, it whirled and swam away and then back again, back and forth. Others came. The curious one came closer. When it went down again, Father stood up and braced himself. The porpoise appeared, very close to the canoe, and Father was ready. With a mighty thrust the spear point found its mark.

"The floats!" cried Father. And Swaloos was ready and pushed them overboard. Already the porpoise had disappeared, dragging the float cord but soon the floats bobbed up again. The porpoise swam about madly. The hunters could follow its course by watching the floats, and paddling after them.

Other men had thrust spears, too. This looked like a fine catch. There was much excitement.

The floats kept the porpoises from staying under water and hindered their swimming, making them tire quickly. When the porpoise was very tired and could no longer fight, Father brought it alongside the dugout. He tipped the canoe and rolled the glistening black body into it, and the cold water rushed in, too. The boy saw the whitish underside as the big fish rolled into the dugout.

"Bail!" Father cried to the boy, and he bailed as fast as he could while Father paddled for shore. The other canoes were following. The rest of the porpoise had quickly disappeared.

The dipper used for bailing was made of a piece of cedar bark cut about three hand lengths long. It was creased across, about one hand length in from each end, then bent up. Each end was gathered around a wooden cross handle

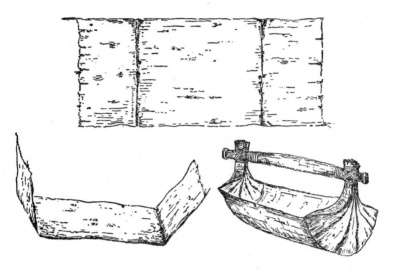

CEDAR BARK CANOE BAILER

and wrapped to stay in place. It made a little basket-like dipper. Swaloos held the bailer by the handle and scooped water out of the canoe.

There was much excitement when they arrived at their village. Every one was pleased over the fine catch. The small boys gathered around Swaloos and admired him. He had been the first of them to go out for porpoise. But Swaloos did not strut nor boast, though he was very proud. He did not forget that he was the grandson of a chief. Such things came as part of the honored position he held. His young friends would not think kindly of him if he boasted.

Others helped Father carry his porpoise up from the beach. Grandfather brought out his drum and beat a song message to his people. He invited all to share the porpoise feast.

Mother and Grandmother began preparations for the feast. Other women came to help. Early that morning Mother had built a fire in the pit and had kept it burning, heating rocks to cook the porpoise should Father bring one. Now the fire was taken from the pit and a layer of seaweed spread on. Then the cleaned porpoise was placed on the hot stones. Quickly, they spread on another layer of seaweed and sprinkled water over all, then more seaweed and the cooking mats. Sand was spread over, then the fire replaced, and more wood piled on. They must wait while the big fish cooked in the pit.

Men sat about talking of other times when big porpoise had visited their waters. The children played.

The rain had stopped and the warm sun was out. The Great-Man smiled down upon the Indian village.

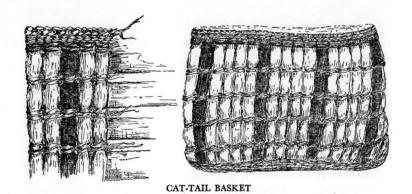

CAT-TAIL BASKET

Chapter XXV

WINTER ON ITS WAY

GRANDMOTHER AND THE LITTLE GIRL spent much time with their weaving. Malitsa watched while Grandmother made baskets of cat-tail leaves. The leaves had been cured in the sun and were now light brown colored. The tough outer edge of the long slender leaves were ripped off first. Grandmother took the long threads from the edges and rolled them on her thigh to twist them into a strong cord. The cord was used to weave the cat-tail leaves together.

The old lady placed the long cat-tail leaves for the basket, then started in the center to make the bottom. Over and under, over and under, until she had woven a square the size she desired for the bottom. Then she turned the rest of each leaf up and these formed the sides. With more cat-tail leaves and cord she wove in and out and tied. The basket soon took shape.

"Oh, Grandmother, I could never do that," Malitsa said wistfully.

Grandmother laughed. "Oh, yes, it is very simple once you have learned. Be patient, little one." The old lady could remember when she had been a child watching her grandmother. "Now watch while I bind the top edge to make it strong." And with the cord she bound and tied until she had a finished design around the top edge.

Some day soon Grandmother would teach Malitsa how to make cat-tail mats. The work on the mats began something like the cat-tail basket work. The tough edges were slipped off for cord. Now the difficult work began. The leaves were spread out flat and then placed so one side of each leaf overlapped another leaf. This would make the finished mat waterproof. Then with the cat-tail cord and a yew wood needle, the leaves were made secure with a row of stitching. A space was left and another row of stitching, and so on until the full length of the leaves was reached. The finished mat was many layers of leaves thick.

A small wooden tool was used to crease and press down along the stitching. The tool was carved and decorated.

The edges of the mats were finished with the cord. Different designs of edgings were used, depending upon the use of that particular mat. The mats that were to be used for bedding had fancy designs. Those to be used for summer shelter were made large and the finished edge was woven extra strong. These would have harder usage than most mats, and would be exposed to the weather. Extra large mats were made to be used for partitions and to line the houses against the winter cold.

There were mats to be spread on the ground at meal time. And those to sit on. Some were used for capes and some to spread across the lap in a canoe. Some were used to spread out in the bottom of the canoe to kneel on or sit on while in the canoe.

But most important was the cat-tail mat for bedding. Many mats were put down to make the beds soft and springy.

For some time Malitsa must be content to learn the

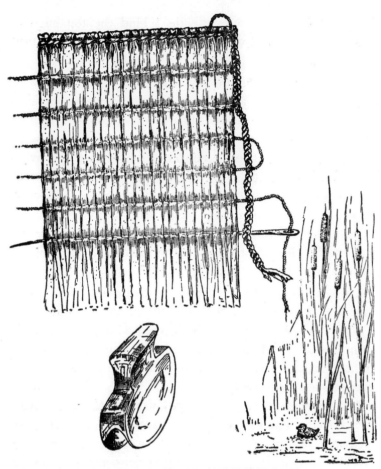

DETAIL OF CAT-TAIL MAT AND CREASING TOOL

simple weaving. As she became older, Grandmother would show her more difficult work.

The sun cast a long golden path across the water to the Indian village. A noise, high overhead, caused the Indians to stop their work and listen. They turned their faces upward, searching the sky.

There, high above was a wedge of flying birds. The nose of the wedge led a direct course toward the south. They called one another as they flew.

"Geese," said Grandfather. "Winter will soon be upon us. The geese are flying south."

The children watched the birds and listened to the old people talk. They told of times when the geese had come by very early. Great numbers of them had flown over. And winter had come soon after. The geese knew, they said, when to expect snow.

Another year the geese had not come until the sun had swung a way to the south. That winter had been mild. There was very little cold. And soon the geese had come by on their way north again.

This winter would be ordinary, the old people said. This was about the right time for the geese to fly. And those birds did not seem to be in a hurry.

Many more flocks of geese would go by, and ducks, too. All traveling birds would point their heads south toward the warmth. The Indians would have plenty of bird meat. There would be feathers for use, too.

Grandfather said sometimes a great flock of geese would arrive as the sun hid itself behind the distant islands. The flock would break up their wedge and circle round and round, calling very loudly. Then, noisily flapping their heavy wings, they would settle down on the marshlands not far from the Indian village. The men would go with their bows and small headed arrows to bring back geese for a feast.

It was easy to find the geese for they honked and made a great commotion while settling themselves for the night. The Indians could easily creep through the brush until close enough to aim their arrows for a perfect shot.

Swaloos hoped a great flock would choose the marshland this season so he might be allowed to go with the men. "It must be wonderful to be a man," he thought.

Swaloos left the village and walked along the path to the stream. He wanted to think of the geese flying and of winter coming.

He noticed how the woods prepared for winter. The trees and bushes could not follow the warmth as the birds did and so they went to sleep.

The vine maple had said goodbye to its bright red leaves as one by one they fluttered to the ground. A red blanket of leaves covered the feet of the mother tree. Swaloos remembered his grandfather had told him the sap would settle down into the roots. It would stay in the roots and the tree would sleep through the cold of winter.

Later, warm spring breezes would awaken the tree. Again the sap would flow upward into even the smallest twigs to feed leaf buds. The sap brought renewed life and tiny new leaves would unfurl and spread open to the sunlight.

Swaloos saw how the alder leaves had all turned yellow. Most of the alder leaves had left the tree. The tall cottonwoods were almost bare. A breeze stirred the leaves still clinging to the trees, and they clacked dryly.

In the spring, when the sap again flowed up in the alder trees, and the buds were fat and red, the older boys and girls would sing the sap eating song. With sticks they would beat a rhythm on the trunk of the alder tree, singing as they tapped. Soon the bruised trunk would yield its sap and between beats the singers would lick the sap from their sticks. The small children tried to imitate their older brothers and sisters but they could not make enough sap come to their sticks.

The giant evergreens, the firs, cedars, spruce and hemlock trees, held their green needles. They did not become bare during the winter. Their cones were turning brown. Swaloos knew their sap was also going into the roots. And soon the strong autumn winds would shake the brown cones loose from the trees. Then the evergreens with their green needles would also rest during the winter.

Many of the animals had made beds and would soon crawl into them for their long winter sleep. Swaloos knew the bears would climb into hollow trees or crawl into fallen dead trees which were hollow, and stay there until spring. Right now the bears were round and fat and well fed. But they would not eat during the winter and when they came out in the spring they would be thin and hungry.

The chipmunks had made nests of dry grass and moss and leaves. They had stored away nuts and cones to nibble on during the winter.

But the deer did not go to sleep for the time of the cold. They roamed the forest and browsed on the winter buds of shrubs and trees.

Swaloos wondered why some animals went to sleep and some did not. He knew the Great-Man had a reason. He wished he knew it.

The boy heard the stream before he could see it. It sounded joyful. Swaloos stood and watched the water tumble and roll over the rocks. The stream was no longer thirsty and weak. It was fat and well-fed from the rains that had come. It would continue to grow until it filled its banks.

Swaloos sat down to listen and think. He felt like singing the farewell song of his people. The trees and animals were going to sleep. The birds were flying to the south. The creek was going to the sea.

Chapter XXVI

DUCKS FLY SOUTHWARD

DAY AFTER DAY great flocks of ducks flew over on their way south. Some circled and settled down on the water near the Indian village. Their noisy calling disturbed the quietness. In the morning, the whirred clapping of many wings told the Indians the ducks were lifting into flight. They would circle and form their flying wedge, heading its point southward.

The Indians had many roast ducks during that time. A duck was mounted on a stick and stood by the fire to roast. As it roasted, Mother turned the duck to brown it all around.

The feathers were saved. The downy ones were used in making yarn. The heavier feathers were peeled away from the quill and then beaten to soften them. The best ones were used in decoration. The brightly colored feathers of mallards were saved for trimmings.

"How can you make yarn of the feathers?" Malitsa asked her grandmother.

"Remember how you rolled the nettle bark threads on your thigh?" Grandmother asked in reply.

"Yes," Malitsa answered her, "but feathers are so short."

Grandmother smiled. Then she told Malitsa how she would spin the yarn. The soft duck feathers would be twirled in with long soft threads of cedar bark and some goat hair or down from fireweed. Grandmother worked them together by rolling them on her thigh.

"We will use the yarn to weave blankets, head bands, and bands for pack straps," Grandmother told Malitsa. "Sometimes we make dye and color the yarn."

"I like pretty colors," said Malitsa. "I want to learn how to dye yarn."

"Later I will show you," Grandmother told her.

Swaloos came running and said to Malitsa, "Oh, sister, Father says I may go with him to hunt ducks tonight. I am so excited."

That night after the darkness had come, Swaloos went with his father in the canoe. They had a burning torch in the stern of the dugout. Swaloos sat back and paddled for his father. Father sat up in the bow. As the canoe floated along slowly the ducks saw the light. They were curious and watched. It was dark where Father sat and they did not see him. Swaloos paddled up close. Father had a long pole with a net fastened to it. He reached out with his pole and caught the ducks while they watched the light.

Swaloos was so excited every time his father caught a duck. He wanted to shout in excitement but he did not. He knew the hunter never makes any noise. So he paddled along, dipping his paddle as silently as possible.

When Father had caught plenty of ducks they turned their dugout toward home.

"We shall have a feast of duck," Father told the boy.

Swaloos was proud. He had helped his father. He was helping to provide a feast for his relatives. Father was paddling now and Swaloos was curled up in the bow. He was thinking. The gentle waves rocked the Indian dugout. Swaloos did not know when his thoughts stopped and his dreams began.

The canoe bottom grated on the shore as Father pushed it to land. Swaloos was startled from his sleep.

"Did you have pleasant dreams?" Father asked, smiling. He remembered when he had been a boy. He used to fall asleep, too, after he had been out with his father to get ducks.

"Oh, yes," Swaloos replied. "I dreamed I was a great

chief. I dreamed all the people liked me. My people were very happy."

"Ah," said Father. "That is a good omen. Some day that dream will come true."

Swaloos went to his bed smiling. They had had good luck with their duck hunting. And he had had a good luck dream.

The sun came up from behind the trees and looked down on the Indian village. Mother and Grandmother would soon begin their preparations for the duck feast. Other women would help them.

Malitsa helped so she could learn about feathers. Grandmother showed Malitsa which were the downy ones and which were heavier. There would be many feathers for Mother and Grandmother to use. Father would choose some to mount on the shafts of his arrows. Some would be saved to decorate drums, rattles, head-dresses and other belongings of the Indians.

Mother built a fire in the cooking pit. Large stones were put in the bottom of the pit. Mother kept the fire burning until the rocks were very hot. Then she removed the fire. The clean ducks were put into the hot pit and surrounded by salal leaves. Water was sprinkled over all. Then a covering of seaweed was spread over to hold the steam inside. The steam and hot rocks cooked the birds, while a fire burned over the covered pit.

All the relatives were glad to share the roast ducks. Swaloos was proud and helped serve the meal. He liked to see the smiles on the faces of his people. He would remember this day for a long time. He felt older now.

Swaloos listened to his father and grandfather talk. They were making plans to put out the duck nets. The duck nets were made of cord Grandmother had spun from nettle bark. She had knotted the long cords to make a strong fine net.

The men knew a special feeding ground where many ducks went to feed. Father would take the duck net to this place. He would spread the net in shallow water. Stone sinkers were fastened to the net. The sinkers would hold it just under the water. It could not be easily seen by the ducks. Father would anchor the net and then leave it.

When the ducks came to feed, they dived to feed on the bottom. They would become tangled in the net and could not get away. Later Father would go back to remove the ducks he had caught in the net.

Chapter XXVII

CEDAR BARK USES

GRANDMOTHER SAT COMBING HER LONG HAIR which hung loosely about her shoulders. The yew wood comb had finger length teeth, thin but strong. When she had finished she called to Malitsa, "Come, let me comb your hair."

The girl hurried to her. She liked to have Grandmother fix her hair. She combed and combed and smoothed the hair back from Malitsa's forehead. She rubbed and rubbed to make it stay in place. And then she braided the beautiful black hair. Malitsa did not like that so well for Grandmother must braid it very tightly to make it grow faster. That pulled and sometimes hurt.

Grandmother also rubbed Malitsa's eyebrows to make them smooth and even. Nice eyebrows were very important to the men as well as the women. It was a sign of beauty.

"Soon you will be old enough to learn many secrets of beauty," Grandmother told Malitsa. The girl was very pleased. "Each time we wash your hair we will braid heliotrope into it so it will smell nice."

Grandmother brought some elk tallow for Malitsa's skin. "Rub it in well," she said, "for it makes the skin soft."

The aged woman showed Malitsa how to rub red paint near her eyes to make them pretty and sparkling. The red paint should also be rubbed into the part of the hair.

"All these will make you more beautiful," the old lady said. "When you are older you must be very careful how you look. Some day a handsome man may come to visit the village and see you."

Malitsa lowered her head. She felt shy when her grandmother said such things.

"How would you like to have me teach you more about cedar bark today?" Grandmother asked.

"Oh, will you?" cried the girl. "I would be so happy to learn."

"Then that is what we will do," Grandmother said. She went into the house and soon returned with a pack of cedar bark. She unfolded a long strip of bark.

"It is wet," observed Malitsa.

"Yes," Grandmother replied. "The cedar bark has soaked in water all night to soften it. If it were not soaked it would break and tear. We want it to bend easily. We want it to come off in long strips."

The old lady taught her granddaughter how to hold the cedar bark and peel the layers. The rough outer bark was laid aside for making baskets and mats.

The soft smooth inner bark which had been close to the tree was used for clothing, thread, yarn, cord and rope. This had to be beaten before it was ready for use. The bark for ropes and cord was beaten slightly, but for clothing, thread or yarn, it must be made soft. Bark used for padding in cradles was pounded until it was as soft as feathers. Beaten cedar bark was also used in fire making, for towels and napkins, and sometimes for cleaning the dishes.

The tool used for pounding the cedar bark was made of whale bone or hardwood, with colored decorations on it. The

CEDAR BARK POUNDER MADE OF WHALE BONE OR HARDWOOD

edge was blunt so it would break the stiffness of the bark without cutting it. Strips of bark were laid across a rock and beaten in a chopping motion with the tool.

Grandmother told Malitsa about making clothing. The long, narrow ribbons of soft cedar bark were tied in certain ways to make dresses, skirts and capes, leaving the ends to hang in fringe. The men and boys, as well as the women and girls, wore knee length skirts and capes made from the cedar bark ribbons.

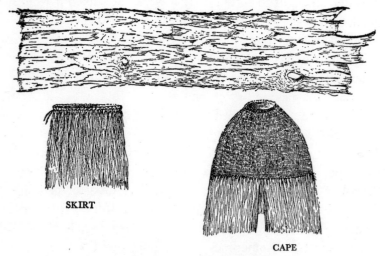

SKIRT

CAPE

SECTION OF SLAB OF CEDAR BARK
The Indians put away piles of these slabs for later use
CEDAR BARK SKIRT AND CAPE

Some of the soft cedar bark was spun with wool or feathers into yarn. It was then woven to make some of their clothes and baskets. Some was also used for weaving long belts which were wrapped around the waist many times to hold the skirts or trousers in place. The men wore trousers when hunting. Both men and women had leggings made from the cedar bark or woven from yarn.

Their very best clothes were made of hides. The moccasins were of buckskin. The clothes made from skins were

(140)

decorated with bone beads, shells, claws, animal teeth or dried deer hoofs. There were also leggings made from buckskin.

Grandmother showed Malitsa how their head bands were woven from cedar bark cord and yarn.

"Could I make one now, Grandmother?" asked Malitsa.

"Yes," Grandmother answered. She was glad to have the girl so interested in learning to make things.

The old lady took some fine cords of cedar bark the length she wanted, and looped them over a framework of small poles which she had standing in the ground for that purpose. Then she gave Malitsa some yarn and showed her how to weave the yarn in and out through the cords.

The child was very pleased with her work. When she had finished the head band she pinned it around her head. Then she ran to find a pretty feather she had saved.

"Now, look, Grandmother," said Malitsa when she had the feather fixed just right.

"That looks fine," said Grandmother, smiling.

"May I make one for Swaloos to surprise him?" the girl wanted to know. Grandmother said she might, and helped her lay out the band, then Malitsa finished it.

When the band was ready she gave it to Swaloos.

"I made it myself," she told him.

"I bet you did not," he said, smiling with pleasure.

"Yes, I did. You ask Grandmother," Malitsa said to prove it.

While these two children learned, other children in the village were being taught by their parents or relatives, also. Each family passed on to the children the knowledge they had gained. In this way the children knew what had taken place before.

During the long winter evenings the men and boys often gathered in the home of an old man. He had to be a good story teller. He told them the tales of hunting and the legends of their forefathers. The girls learned the stories of the tribe from the old women.

Swaloos and his friends were proud to be able to join the men. They listened to every word. But the stories went on and on. One by one the boys' heads nodded and dropped. Sleep surrounded them and the stories went on in their dreams.

Chapter XXVIII

WOOD CARVING

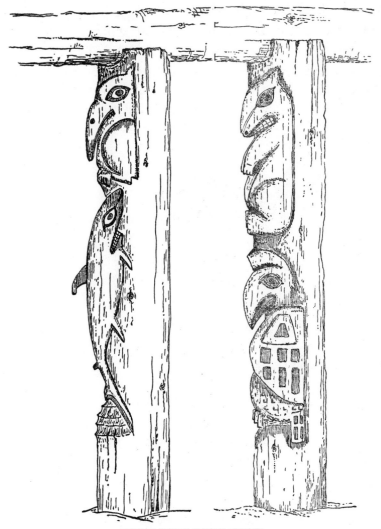

TOTEM POSTS INSIDE HOUSE

THE OLD GRANDFATHER was a very fine carver. He carved

many articles from wood. There were the beautiful long canoes and the totem posts carved from cedar trees. The totem posts stood inside the house. They were carved and painted with figures of birds, fish, or animals. The figures on the posts told legends or stories of the family. Most of the stories were lessons on bravery, goodness, cleanliness and other behavior, and showed what evil came from bad behavior.

There were also many other articles carved from cedar. Grandfather made wooden ducks, small ones to be used for ceremonial rattles and larger ones for fishing floats and

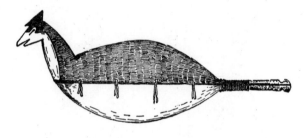

CEREMONIAL RATTLE

decoys for duck hunting. They were hollow inside. The rattles had small pebbles in them so they could be shaken in time to the music.

Maple wood had many uses in carving. Dishes were made by hollowing the inside and carving the outside of a piece of maple. After it was hollowed and smoothed to suit, the dish was painted with designs. Some of these dishes were very large. Grandfather had spoons he had carved from maple. The handles of some had very fine carvings of animals or birds. These spoons were used to dip the food from the large dishes. Smaller wooden paddle-like spoons were used to push the food from the larger spoon into the mouth.

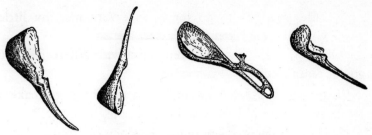

CARVED HORN AND WOODEN SPOONS

A canoe bailer, shaped square and bell-like, was carved from maple.

Swaloos liked to use his grandfather's tools. There was an elk horn chisel. Another chisel had a horn handle and stone blade made secure with wrappings. There was also a chisel of stone. The wedges were of elk horn and hardened wood. Stone hammers and stone mallets were used. A stone work axe had a wooden handle. The handle had been split so that a half went on each side of the axe blade. The handle was bound to the stone blade by split cedar root thongs. The thongs had been bound on while wet and left to dry. As it dried it would shrink and hold very tight.

The adz, which Grandfather used especially on canoes, was a stone blade with a whale-bone handle. The blade had been sharpened and polished. Grandfather knew secrets about sharpening and polishing tools and weapons. Some day he would teach all these secrets to Swaloos. The boy could hardly wait to learn. He loved the tools and was anxious to make things with them.

Grandfather was pleased that the boy wanted to learn. A good worker was always held in high regard by his people. Each person in the village tried to do his best so the others would think well of him. A lazy person was looked down upon. The chief must do extra good work. He was the leader. He was the one to guide the others. He must be kind, yet strong and manly.

"Would you like to go for a walk with me, my little son?" Grandfather asked, one day.

"Oh, yes," the boy answered, quickly. "Where are you going, Grandfather?"

"I am going to scout around for a cedar tree to make a big dugout," the old man replied. "Come, let us go."

The boy followed his grandfather along the trail and into the woods. They had not gone far when Swaloos exclaimed, "There is a big cedar tree. How would that one do?"

"It would not do at all," the old man said. "See how the bark seems to grow twisted around the tree? The grain of the wood inside the bark is also twisted. If we tried to split the wood of that tree it would split crookedly. We must find a tree with the lines of the bark growing straight up."

They walked on through the woods. Swaloos watched his grandfather. He wanted to learn to be like him. The old man stopped before a tall cedar. Swaloos looked at the bark.

"This one has straight grained bark," the boy said. "Do you think it would make a good canoe?"

"Yes, the grain of the bark is straight," Grandfather replied, "but the tree is not a good one for our purpose. This is the male tree. We know it by the growth of the limbs. The male tree is strong and holds its limbs so they grow up. But that shows the wood is tough. Tough wood is hard to carve."

Swaloos followed his grandfather as he walked in and out among the trees. Finally the old man came to a tall cedar. He examined it. He walked around the tree, looking at it. The boy kept silent. He felt this must be a good tree.

"This is a fine tree," Grandfather said, at last. "This is a female tree. See how the limbs droop? That shows the wood is soft. It is so soft the tree can not hold its limbs up. Their weight bends them down. The grain will be fine and pink colored. The wood of the male tree is yellow colored."

"How do you know all these things, Grandfather?" the boy asked, bewildered.

The old man answered, "Through many years I have watched and listened and remembered."

"I want to do that, too," Swaloos said. "I am going to start right now to remember all I see and hear."

"There will be many things you see and hear which will be better forgotten," said the wise old Chief. "You will have to choose. But what you have seen and heard today will be well to remember."

Swaloos knew he would not forget this walk with his grandfather.

"Now I will mark this tree," said the old man. "Later the tree will be cut. We will all gather for the tree-cutting ceremony. Then the work with the adz will begin. You may help me this year, my little grandson."

"Oh, Grandfather!" Swaloos cried, "I am so happy!" He wanted to shout and dance but he must be dignified, he reminded himself.

Chapter XXIX

MALITSA LEARNS MANY THINGS

EACH DAY MALITSA SAT WITH HER GRANDMOTHER. The old lady was teaching her the secrets of making baskets. Some other women in the village made baskets, too, but only the old wife of the Chief could make the perfect water-tight ones.

Malitsa must first learn to make ordinary baskets well. Then Grandmother would show her how to make the water-tight ones. She would also teach her other weaving. But she was young yet and there would be plenty of time to learn all the secrets. Her lessons would go on for many seasons.

The Indians needed many baskets. They were used for storing winter food, for cooking, for gathering berries and clams, for carrying water, as well as for many other uses.

Grandmother showed Malitsa how to shape a basket from the very tiny limbs of the cedar tree. Mother had gone to a swampy place where the moisture fed the trees and made them grow fast. She had gathered the long, slender limbs and roots of the cedars and brought them home for winter work. Now Grandmother and the girl were using some of the limbs.

The materials had been soaked in water to soften. The limbs were split in half.

First a flat bottom was woven strongly. Then the sides were shaped of tiny split limbs, spaced apart to leave openings so the finished basket would be open-work. Some baskets had larger open-work than others because of the different uses of the baskets. The sides were held in shape by lacings of strong cedar root, split thin. The rows of lacings were also spaced apart.

(148)

The cedar root had been split into narrow ribbon-like strips, long and thin, but very strong. This split cedar root had many other uses besides basket making.

Grandmother told Malitsa how to weave around the top edge. The design was for beauty as well as strength. These baskets must be strong, especially the clam baskets, for they would be filled with heavy loads of freshly dug clams. When these baskets of clams were washed the sand could wash out through the open-work.

There were different designs for the sides of these baskets. Sometimes Grandmother peeled the thin bark from the limbs before using them. Other times she peeled part of the limbs and used a peeled one and then one with the bark on. This made light and dark colored stripes on the finished basket.

Some of the baskets had handles on each side and some had strong handles across their tops.

Malitsa was very proud of her first basket of split cedar limbs. She asked Mother to use her basket for carrying clams next time.

Mother looked at Malitsa's work and was pleased with how well she had done. Mother could make baskets, too, but the grandmothers usually taught the children. They were older and much wiser. They could not do the hard work and so they were the teachers.

"Grandmother," said Malitsa while they were at work one day, "sometimes I think the boys and men do the most important work."

"Oh, no, my little one," Grandmother said quickly, "that is not right."

"They go hunting and fishing," said Malitsa. "They go away in canoes. They have bows and arrows to guard against the enemy."

"Think, my child," Grandmother replied, "of the work of the women. They cook and feed the men and children.

They make all the clothes. They prepare the food for winter. They care for the children and tend the home."

"Yes," said Malitsa, thinking of all the work her mother did about the village.

"A woman's hands are very important," the wise Grandmother told the child. "Remember, in your hands you carry many blessings. With your hands you do many things for your family. A woman's work is as important as a man's. But, both must work together for happiness. Never forget that."

Malitsa sighed. "I will remember that always, Grandmother. You make things seem just right."

"And always be happy with your work," advised Grandmother, "and good luck will be with you."

The girl kept thinking of these things Grandmother had told her, even after she had gone to play.

One day a strange odor drifted up from a large cooking basket. Malitsa did not remember that odor.

"What are you cooking, Grandmother?" Malitsa asked.

"I am not cooking," Grandmother replied. "I am making dye."

Malitsa watched with interest. The old lady explained how dyes were made and showed her granddaughter how to make them.

"This is a brown dye," she explained. "It is made from little frog skirts."

"Frog skirts?" echoed the child.

"Yes," laughed Grandmother, "they are fungi which grow on the maple tree. We gather them and boil them to make brown color. Other barks and roots make different colors. A dark red dye is made from boiled hemlock bark. Boiled grape root makes a yellow color."

Grandmother told her how she used the strong dye for darker or brighter shades. Lighter shades were made by adding more water to the dye to weaken it.

When dyeing wool or basket grasses, Grandmother let it stand in the dye water until it was the shade of color she wanted. She told Malitsa many secrets of making dyes.

"But how is a canoe dyed?" asked Malitsa.

Grandmother smiled before she answered. "The canoe is not dyed, Malitsa. It is painted. Surely you remember about that. The totem posts are painted, too. Also the designs on wooden articles, like dishes of maple, and wooden spoons."

"Oh, yes, I remember now that paint was made with salmon eggs and colored powder," said Malitsa, feeling a little foolish for having forgotten about seeing Father painting his new canoe.

Grandmother had finished boiling her dye and she set it aside to cool.

Malitsa was looking about for something to do. She saw a young mother going to her house. Malitsa liked babies and she went over to see the tiny son of Fine-Feathers.

Fine-Feathers took the baby out of his cradle. She put him on a cat-tail mat. Fine-Feathers showed Malitsa the correct way to rub the baby's arms and legs and body.

"It is to make him strong," the young mother explained, "and to give him a well shaped body."

She also rubbed his hair to make it grow back from his face. She rubbed his eyebrows to give them the right shape. Then very carefully she lifted him back into his cradle.

"We do not handle the baby often," Fine-Feathers explained. "Lifting and carrying a baby is not good for his body. His cradle or baby-board keeps his body growing right."

Fine-Feathers showed Malitsa how the cradle was padded with very finely shredded cedar bark to make it soft. The padding was placed to fit the baby's body. A soft blanket of goat wool kept the baby warm.

When the baby was tucked into his cradle Fine-Feathers

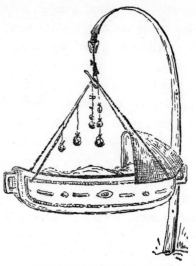

CRADLE ON YEW WOOD SWING

took the cradle back to its swing. The swing was a long yew wood pole split in half. Yew wood is very strong and tough. The large end of the pole was buried in the ground at an angle. The cradle was fastened to the other end, swinging as if on a spring. A cord was fastened so the mother could swing the cradle from where she sat at her work.

Malitsa asked Fine-Feathers if she might rock the baby. The young mother let her teeter the cradle and soon the baby was asleep. Malitsa tiptoed out of the house.

She walked softly, daintily, her fringed skirt swaying gently. She carried her head high, her beautiful black hair smoothed back in long braids. She was happy. Grandmother was teaching her so many new secrets. It made her proud to be a girl. If she learned all her lessons well, she would be worthy some day of becoming the wife of a chief.

As Malitsa came near her house she saw that Grandmother and Mother had been watching her. They had spoken to one another while looking at her. Malitsa wondered what they had been saying. And when she came close something in their eyes gave the answer even before Grand-mother spoke.

"My little one, we are very proud of you," the old lady said gently.

Chapter XXX

SEARCHING FOR THE TOTEM SPIRIT

ONE EVENING THE INDIANS HAD SETTLED around their fires. Swaloos felt a singing within himself. He was happy. He felt excitement as if something good were going to happen. Nothing had happened during the day to make him feel this way. Though he had seen his father and grandfather talking together, in very low tones. And they had barely glanced at him once while they talked.

Now as the little night breezes blew the last daylight out across the salt water toward the sun's bed, the heart of Swaloos seemed to grow large. It seemed to crowd inside his chest.

"Come, my son," Grandfather said to Swaloos, and the boy was startled. But only for an instant. He went quickly to stand before his grandfather where he sat beside Father. His heart beat loudly within him. He knew his grandfather was going to give him an order of importance.

"Yes, Grandfather," Swaloos said, standing straight as a young cedar sapling.

"Tonight, my boy," Grandfather spoke quietly so no others about the fire might hear, "I want you to go to yonder point." He paused, searching the boy's face. Then he continued. "You are to take the totem stick and leave it. You are to sit and think. Then you must go into the water and bathe. When you come out of the water, rub your body well with sand. That will make you strong and manly.

The boy stood straight and held his head up proudly. He knew the meaning of these orders. He knew someday while on such a journey his totem spirit would speak to him. The totem spirit would come in the form of an animal or a bird

or a fish. Whichever it might be, it would be his guiding
spirit throughout his life. That would be his totem. It would
watch over him and care for him. And when he grew to
manhood he would carve his guardian spirit on his own
totem post inside the house.

"Here is the totem stick," said Grandfather, giving
Swaloos a stick with many carvings upon it. The boy's hand
trembled as he reached for the treasured stick. "If you
should hear a voice do not be frightened. Stay and listen to
what it tells you. Do not let anyone see you leaving the
village. Do not tell anyone what you see or hear. That
would be ill luck. Now, go my young chief, and may the
good spirits of our people guide you and watch over you."

"Yes, sir," breathed Swaloos, so great was his excitement.

He wanted to run from the house but no, he must go
slowly, in no hurry. He must hold back his feet, for they
wanted to carry him away as if on wings. The boy glanced
about the room and saw that his relatives were busy. No one
paid him any attention. Each step pulled him toward the
door. He hoped the vine maple hinge would be silent for
this one time. He liked its merry song as it sang a welcome
or farewell to whoever passed through the door. Tonight,
just this one night, he hoped it would be still.

Swaloos pushed gently upon the heavy cedar planked
door. It gave to his touch and the hinges whispered softly as
the door swung. It seemed to say, "Swaloos, Swaloos," and
as the door closed behind him he heard it say, "Good luck,
good luck."

For a moment the boy stood still in the shadow, listening,
watching. His eyes searched to be sure no other person in
the village might see him. When he was certain he was the
only one about, he darted quickly to the path leading toward
the point. As soon as he knew he was out of sight he stopped,
again listening. Now he felt all alone.

Swaloos drew in a deep, deep breath and lifted his arms

wide. The moon rode out brightly from behind a cloud. To the north, to the south, to the east and to the west, the young Indian breathed deeply and spread his arms welcoming his guardian spirit. He urged it to come. To come and speak to him on this night.

Then with quick, bounding leaps, arms outstretched, he went toward the point. He seemed to grow stronger. His leaps were broader and at times he seemed to be sailing, soaring with the clouds. He laughed and grasped the totem stick harder in his hand. It might come to him tonight.

"Come, my spirit, come," he chanted softly. "Speak to me."

But no voice came. He must not give up yet. He had only just begun. The path led him out onto the beach. Here the evergreens grew close on a point of land stretched toward the great wide water. Here a dead snag of an ancient cedar stood dark against the sky.

An old tide-washed tree lay upon the beach. Swaloos sat down on it to think. His thoughts carried him far away into the stories of his grandfather. He remembered the brave men who had lived before him. He called them by name, but he heard no answer.

Leaving the totem stick upon the old tree, he again ran with leaps and bounds, his arms flung wide in happiness. He ran to the water and dived under its green-black surface. As he swam, golden bubbles slipped off his body and made a trail behind him. The almost icy coldness nipped and stung his body. A silver path led across the water to the moon and he followed it out a little way, then turned and swam back to shore.

Quickly he dug his hands into the sand and rubbed it on his body. This made him clean and strong. With spreading arms and light feet he ran back to him totem stick. He sat down, took up the stick and by the light of the moon studied the carvings on it. Each figure game him a feeling of great

(156)

strength and power. He followed the carvings with his finger. He let his thoughts go soaring again, hunting for his own spirit, wishing it would come to him.

"But I am much too young," he told himself. "I can not expect it so soon. Grandfather says sometimes it takes many, many moons before a totem spirit settles down upon the body and makes it his own. I must come many times and call to my guardian. Some day he will answer. He will talk to me and then I will know. But until that time comes I must go on searching for my guardian spirit."

A fluttering rustle of feathers broke into Swaloos' thoughts. He glanced about him. He could see nothing at all. His heart beat fast. Could it be his guardian spirit near? No. He told himself it was too soon.

Again he heard rustling feathers. This time he was sure he had heard it truly and not in his thoughts. He looked all about him. His face turned toward the dead cedar snag. There high on a limb he saw something dark move slightly. He watched. Moonlight caught the white head of a mighty eagle as he stretched one long wing and then the other. The huge bird shook himself to straighten his feathers, and settled back on his limb to sleep.

Swaloos' eyes filled with wonderment. "I wonder," he whispered softly, "I wonder. No, I must not think of it. It is the eagle, the mighty hunter, waiting for dawn."

The boy sat quietly for some time, then he placed the totem stick where it would be safe, so Grandfather would know that he had been to the point. He went back along the path to his house. He ran lightly, happily, his head up and his face smiling. A voice inside him warned not to tell of seeing the eagle.

Very quietly Swaloos slipped through the door, the vine maple hinge barely whispering so he could not hear the song. He made his way to his bed and crept under the covers.

It was then that sleep settled down upon all the household.

Chapter XXXI

INVITATION TO A POTLATCH

THE TWO CHILDREN SAW their grandfather taking down his big drum. It had a wooden frame with buckskin stretched tightly across and bound so it would hold. They knew there would be a message to the people and were anxious to hear it. Grandfather went out of the house and the children followed.

The Chief stood beside his door and with the buckskin padded drumstick, beat a quick rhythm. The drum boomed, its big voice reaching out to every one in the village.

Men and women came from their houses. Some of the women carried babies. Children skipped along ahead of their parents. But there was no noise. The children knew they must be quiet. The men and women knew by the drum song that their chief had an important message.

All the people of the village had gathered before the Chief's house. He stood very straight and dignified, his gray head held high, his brown face wrinkled in lines of kindness. He held out his arms in greeting, and then he spoke in a slow distinct voice.

"My good people, we have had a fine year. The Great-Man has been kind. He has brought us plenty of food. I wish to honor my friends. I shall hold a potlatch when the moon comes full and round."

The members of the tribe looked at one another and smiled. They liked a potlatch.

"I will invite many friends to come to our village," the Chief continued. "For days there will be feasting and dancing and games. I will give many presents in honor of my potlatch."

Swaloos and Malista had heard the old people talk of times when there was a potlatch. They did not remember one. Potlatches were not held often and only then by the wealthy.

"Fleet-of-Foot and Running-With-the-Wind! Son-of-the-Paddle and Man-With-the-Strong-Arm!" the Chief called.

Four men stepped forward, heads high, strong muscles showing beneath copper colored skin. These were the Chief's trusted carriers.

"When the sun again sends his gold and red scouts into the sky be prepared to carry the invitation sticks to my friends in the other villages," the old man said to them.

They bowed their heads in a sign of yes. And their Chief dismissed them with a wave of his hand which meant he depended upon them to be ready. They would not fail him for they had been trained for this work.

"We will begin now to make ready for feasting," the Chief told the other people. "The hunters will go to the woods, fishermen to the sea, and the women will prepare the foods. Winter's cold breath has frosted growing things and the earth. The food will stay cold and ready for use. We must feed our guests well." A few more drum beats and, holding up the drum and stick, the old man signaled that his talk was finished.

The people began to talk over the potlatch plans. Every one was happy.

Early the next morning the four carriers waited for their call. Two canoes were waiting, packed, ready for the journey. Two pack straps held food for a journey on foot.

Tom-tom-tom, the drum song sounded. The carriers went quickly to stand before the Chief. He had the bundles of ironwood invitation sticks. Each stick was as long as the width of a hand, but not as big around as a finger.

"Fleet-of-Foot," the leader said. That man stepped forward. Now he must pay very close attention. The Chief gave him a bundle of sticks, telling him which tribe it meant. Now, slowly, the Chief named each person of that tribe who should be invited. In the bundle was a stick for each person named. Fleet-of-Foot must remember those names. And he would, for he had been trained to remember very well. Another bundle was for another tribe, and each stick a certain person to be invited. And so on.

The Chief gave the orders to one carrier at a time and he left immediately. Fleet-of-Foot and Running-With-the-Wind to the mountains. Son-of-the-Paddle and Man-With-the-Strong-Arm in canoes along the shores and into the mouths of the rivers. One was to go to the north and the other to the south.

Each man would visit the tribes named to him. He must ask for the chief of the tribe, and would be escorted to the chief's house. He had been trained to speak well and he must make a speech telling of the potlatch. With great ceremony he would tell who had sent the invitation sticks, showing a small article belonging to his chief. This was to prove where he had come from and that it was not an enemy trick.

After the carrier made his speech, he untied the bundle of invitation sticks for that tribe. One by one he handed the sticks to that chief, naming to whom each stick should be given.

When he had finished, he immediately went on his way to the next village.

Meanwhile at the home village the people prepared for the coming potlatch. Swaloos and Malitsa could hardly wait for the time to come.

The Chief and his family had been making preparations for this event for a long time. The Chief had planned for many years to give a big potlatch. He had made tools, bows and arrows, and implements. He had carved bowls and spoons and dishes for presents. Grandmother and Mother had made baskets, blankets and other things that would make gifts. They had saved the nicest big white clam shells. There were extra dried foods to be given away.

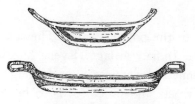

MUCKAMUCK DISHES

Many new dishes, bowls and spoons had been made to serve the guests. There were beautiful new muckamuck dishes in all sizes, carved from maple and decorated with painted designs. They looked like small fat canoes. Soup and other hot foods would be served in these huge dishes. The Chief had carved spoons and bowls from wood. Some had animals carved on the handles. New white clam shells had been saved for bowls to serve their special guests.

As the time for the potlatch drew near, the hunters and fishermen brought in the game. They brought deer meat, ducks and grouse, fish and seal. Much food would be needed, for there would be a great many people. And the Chief must make a big showing before his friends. The people of the village wanted to help. They wanted their leader to be admired.

The children and old ones brought wood and piled it high. Many fires would be needed to cook the food. There would also be fires for the ceremonies and dances. Swaloos and Malitsa carried wood until their arms ached. They felt they must carry more than the others because their grand-father was giving the potlatch.

The women took down the partition mats in the Chief's big house and made one huge room for the occasion. They cleaned and made ready for their guests.

Chapter XXXII

THE POTLATCH

THE FIRST DAY of the potlatch came. The sun was kind and smiled upon the Indian village. Every one was up early. The women fanned their fires into dancing flames. They prepared huge roasts and other foods to be ready to serve the guests when they arrived.

The children were clean and wore their new buckskin clothes. Malitsa was especially proud. She had helped make her own clothes. Grandmother had given her a necklace to wear. Swaloos wore an eagle feather with his headband, and some eagle claws swung on his shirt.

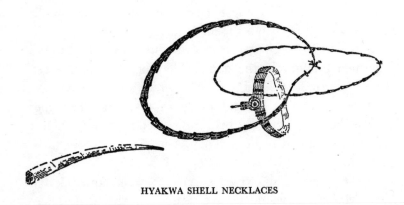

HYAKWA SHELL NECKLACES

Grandmother and Mother wore dresses of white elkskin. They had many necklaces of shells, beads from bone, and white hyakwa shells. Their headbands were many colors woven together and each had a pure white feather.

Grandfather and Father wore white elkskin suits trimmed with beaver teeth and eagle claws. They, too, wore necklaces of hyakwa. Man-With-Piercing-Eyes had a headband of brightly colored yarns and feathers. Chief Carver-of-Wood had many more feathers and tufts of white down, also fur tails, on his headpiece.

The children wished they might have suits of the beautiful soft white skin but the old ones had promised white suits for their naming ceremonies. Such beautiful skin clothing was only for the most special occasions.

Swaloos and Malitsa watched for canoes. Mother, Woman-With-Busy-Hands, directed the last minute food preparations.

The boy was first to see a black spot far out on the water. He felt sure it was the first of their guests. He ran excitedly to tell his grandfather.

Grandfather and his family took their places inside the invitation house. There they would wait the arrival of their guests. The children wished they could be outside to watch. But the host and his family always remained inside the house until the guests came in.

The Chief had asked some young men to go down to the water's edge to greet his friends. They took care of the canoes and paddles, helped the guests with their baskets and bedding rolls.

A welcome dance which expressed happiness and good cheer greeted the guests. They brought gifts of food and useful articles to the Chief. Now the big muckamuck dishes were brought in filled with steaming food. New wooden bowls and spoons were passed to the visitors. They were to help themselves to the food and find a place to sit and eat. Food was kept ready and served immediately to new arrivals.

Many people had landed before darkness covered the village. They were given places inside the big house. They spread their bedding upon the bed shelf and arranged their belongings. Costumes and drums were hung on the wooden pegs in the wall above the bed shelf. Some of the visitors

(163)

stayed in other houses with friends or relatives. But most of the people of the village met in the Chief's invitation house to enjoy the dances and games, and to visit.

Four huge fires were spaced down the center of the long room. Young men brought heavy chunks of wood to pile on the fires. New flames licked out and around the chunks. Smoke, alive with sparks, curled and twisted up and out the open smoke holes in the roof. The air smelled of burning pitch. A faint mist of blue smoke shaded the corners but the bright flames brought out coppery lights on the skins of the people sitting along the sidewalls.

Swaloos and Malitsa sat by Grandfather. The children looked about in awe. So many people, more than they had ever seen at one time.

Malitsa whispered to her brother, "What is the stick Grandfather holds out in front of him, so straight up and down?"

TAMANAWIS STICKS OR POWER STICKS

Said to give great power to one holding it

The boy answered in her ear, "It is the tamanawis stick. Grandfather says it gives power to one who holds it. There is magic in it. See the large clusters of deer hoofs near the top?"

"Yes," his sister whispered back. "I am afraid of it."

Swaloos wanted to show that a boy would not be afraid to touch the magic stick. He put out a venturing finger toward the stick but before his finger quite touched the stick, he jerked his hand back.

"I am afraid of it, too," he admitted to his sister.

"Look, there are other tamanawis sticks," said Malitsa, looking about the room. "Many of the visitors are holding them just like Grandfather does, standing straight with one end resting on the ground, both hands on the stick. I wonder if the magic is coming to them."

DANCER WITH FEATHER HOOD

The Chief passed his tamanawis stick to Father, the dry deer hoof clusters rattling with the slightest movement. He took up his drum and stood, straight and tall. His deep voice raised in song, his great drum beating out a rhythm. His people joined him to sing their friendly welcome song. Soon the tom-tom-tom of drums about the room led voices in the answering song. The very air seemed to beat the rhythm. It went through the bodies and echoed in temples and chests. Then with a final burst, stopped. The vibration seemed to still fill the air. The children waited, hearts beating fast with expectation.

Softly, now, a low tum-tum-tum, calling on the spirit of dance. Tamanawis sticks played their dry song in time with the drums. Pleading, seeking, begging the spirit of dance to come to them. Suddenly a maddening tom-tom-tom filled the air and as many dancers as there are fingers on the hand seemed to come from nowhere. They sprang, legs crouched, arms and fingers spread, palms outward. Up and down, springing, each jump carrying them on around the row of fires. Their bare feet sent up puffs of dust.

Bands of clustered deer hoofs about the ankles, below the knees and on their wrists, clacked in rhythm. The fast, constant rattle of the dry hoofs called for fleetness of foot. Mounted on their buckskin shirts were rows and rows of carved wooden war clubs. They swung in rhythm begging courage for the dancer. Tall hoods, masses of black feathers, bobbed back and forth in time to the music. Where feathers did not cover the faces, black paint was streaked across in finger-wide lines.

Round and round they went, now running with feet lifting high, now vibrating with short low springs in the same spot. Now the arms told the story of the dance, first one up and the other low, then changing. Now turning, slowly, round and round, then faster and faster and faster. Suddenly again the short low springs. Then gaining more speed and out of sight beyond the ring of firelight. With three quick, hard beats the drums ceased.

The air was filled with vengeance and hate for the enemy, as the dance told the story.

Again the coaxing tum-tum-tum-tum and out of the shadows came a slowly swaying figure, covered thickly from head to bare feet with shredded cedar bark. Clusters of dry deer hoofs on the ankles tapped lightly. A low sweet melody rose and drifted, as the curls of blue smoke. Friendship, the arms spread wide and low, then the hands brought up over the heart. Round and round the fires and out again into shadow, the song fading.

A burning chunk broke, sparks and new flames showed smiles and happiness on the faces about the circle.

A low moaning, growling, above the drums and a huge bear skin covered all but the bare feet of a dancer. In and out among the fires he ambled, growling fiercely, then back and out of sight.

THE MONSTROUS BIRD DANCER

The children had thought it a real bear until they saw the feet below the skin. This was fun.

Now the drums thundered, a weird scream, and a monstrous looking bird flapped its long wings. Black feathers covered the body and wings, glistening in the firelight. The dancer began circling the room in rhythmic steps. The head turned from side to side, its long, brightly painted beak reaching beyond arm's length. Its staring, fixed eyes searched for prey. The weird cry broke out above the drums, again and again. Finally the wings folded, the huge beak pointed into the darkness.

A hush held the whole room. The children could still feel prickles on their scalps. The huge eye had seemed to always be looking at them.

Now drums and voices singing a melody like flowing waters. Elk antlers came into view. A slow, rhythmic tap-tap —tap, tap. Below the antlers, a painted body and a skirt of cedar bark ribbons strung with dried hoofs. Step, step . . . step, step, feet lifted high, carefully, very slowly. The gently swaying body tapped dry hoof on dry hoof. In each hand an elk horn point, and at a beat in the rhythm, the points were clicked together. The song died away. Only the low pulsing of the drums and hoofs in rhythmic tap-tap— tap, tap. Now and then a blowing-whistling sound. Slowly on around the fires. Then faster and faster, the song flowing again, faster to the end.

One by one, far into the night, the dancers from different tribes circled the fires, telling their stories in dance and song and drum-beat.

The children fell asleep. They would be up early for games.

In the morning, the older people slept the sun far into the sky. Then they, too, had games, canoe races, swimming and diving, lifting and shooting contests. When darkness came again and the fires burned brightly there were more dances. They sang of love and war and funny songs.

The Chief counted off the days. The sun had come and gone as many times as he had fingers. The last day of the potlatch had come. The old man stood beside his gifts and made a speech to his guests. He told how his guardian spirit had come to him long ago speaking of this great day when he could honor his friends. With all their good fortune in hunting and fishing the Great-Man had helped him, and the day had come to him at last.

Then he called upon his grand-children to dance.

"Do not forget what Grandfather taught us," Malitsa whispered to her brother. "We are to show the guests they have made us glad by coming."

Smiling happily, the children skipped about, their arms spread to show how welcome their friends were. Around the room they went, pausing before each tribe and dancing to them, then going on to the next. The old man was proud of his grand-children.

When they had finished, the Chief began to hand out his gifts. But before presenting the gift, he made a long speech telling good things about the friend. This made every one happy.

Meanwhile outside Grandmother was presenting gifts to her friends who were the wives of the Chief's friends.

All day long this went on. When all the guests had received their gifts, it was time to start homeward. The canoes were loaded. The visitors climbed into their canoes and pushed away from shore.

A sadness seemed to come to the people. Friends were parting. A low song rose above the dip of the paddles. The old Chief and his people sang together. It was the potlatch song of farewell to the gifts, asking them to return two-fold. The Chief hoped his friends would invite him to a big potlatch some day.

The canoes moved outward leaving trails in the water behind them. The Indians on the shore sang the farewell, their bodies gently swaying to the rhythm.